Sir James Goldsmith

Geoffrey Wansell has been a journalist nearly all his working life. He has been a reporter and feature writer on *The Times*; controller of Britain's first commercial radio station; the *Observer*'s diarist Pendennis; and a columnist on Sir James Goldsmith's weekly news magazine *Now!* during the nineteen months of its life.

Born in Scotland in 1945, he is married and has a small son. Although he now writes for *The Times* and for the *Telegraph Sunday Magazine*, he has given up working for any single newspaper or magazine to become a full-time writer.

Geoffrey Wansell

Sir James Goldsmith

Fontana Paperbacks

First published by Fontana Paperbacks 1982

Copyright © Geoffrey Wansell 1982

Set in 10 on 10¼ Plantin
Made and printed in Great Britain
by William Collins Sons & Co. Ltd, Glasgow

For Jan, without whom nothing
would ever have been possible

Contents

Preface

Everyone has an opinion about Sir James Goldsmith. He is adored and detested, acclaimed and despised, but never ignored. For a businessman, even a successful one, it is an extraordinary public reputation. He has been called Machiavellian and misunderstood, a financial buccaneer and a cross between the Master Builder and Houdini, but throughout the forty-nine years of his life he has always provoked a response.

Yet in spite of the controversy and the endless speculation about him, Sir James Goldsmith has remained an enigmatic, indeed a curiously remote figure. Like a great beast he has always avoided coming to the waterhole until dusk. Is he a monster or not?

Even though I worked for him for nearly two years as a columnist on his British weekly news magazine *Now!*, I hardly knew any more about him when it closed than I had when it began. He would appear in the offices from time to time, always cheerful, but looking a little as though he were embarrassed in case anyone should think he might be interfering. At two dinners he gave for his journalists at his house in Richmond he was affable, courteous and entertaining. Not the performance of the man who had become a public figure since his relentlessly publicized libel case against *Private Eye* had begun in 1976. Not the man of the legend.

On Monday, 27 April 1981, when he decided to close the magazine he had launched nineteen months before, I became more than ever determined to try to discover what motivated this extremely public yet still determinedly private man. I knew I did not understand him, but I was also convinced that most of the judgements about him in the British press did not help to understand him either. So I decided to try and find out whether the reality of Sir James Goldsmith matched his public reputation.

Even now, nearly a year later, I am far from certain that

I have grasped the many contradictions that lie at the heart of a man who is now probably one of the richest in Europe and seems intent on becoming one of the richest in the world. But I am convinced that the public stereotype of him as a belligerent, self-seeking tycoon with extreme right-wing opinions is far from the whole truth.

Sir James Goldsmith is probably a mystery even to himself. He has the compulsions and the demons of a man determined to make a reputation and to leave a mark in the world. But I doubt many could honestly say that they have not occasionally shared his desire for wealth and power, even if in their daydreams; just as I doubt that few can view his achievement without some feelings of suspicion or envy. A man who has lived out the private fantasies of so many of us, and done so with such unashamed and public abandon, inevitably invites violent reactions. No group has reacted with more outrage than journalists, and particularly British journalists. So although I began with only one preconception about Sir James Goldsmith – that his was an extraordinary human story which seemed never to have been properly told – the further I went, the more I came to realize that I was also examining the nature of journalism and its power to create myths. For anyone who tries to describe Sir James Goldsmith inevitably finds himself examining the myth that surrounds him and how it came into being.

There seems to be no room for middle ground in any description of him. He is either a hero or a villain. He can never be neither or both. There has hardly been a figure in modern times so persistently judged on the findings of hearsay, and for whom the myth has become almost greater than the reality.

Many of the people whom I should thank for their help in writing this book would only agree to speak to me if I would agree in return never to acknowledge that we had spoken. So any list of acknowledgements I might make would be curiously filleted, and would give undue prominence to the few whom I could name. In the circumstances I have decided not to thank publicly anyone who told me anything about Sir James Goldsmith. Instead I offer them all my profound, humble – but private – thanks.

Nevertheless I must express my gratitude to Marcel Berlins for his encouragement and knowledge of France, Giles Clark for his advice, Stephen du Sautoy for his conviction that the search was worthwhile, Caroline Brakspear for her ability to decipher the manuscript, and my agent Leslie Gardiner for her unwavering support. But most of all I must thank my wife Jan for accepting this book as a constant part of our lives while I was writing it. None of them should be blamed for my conclusions. Those are mine alone.

London, February 1982

Prologue

When Jimmy Goldsmith woke up on that May morning in 1954 the sun was streaming through the curtains of his fifth-floor suite in the Hotel Scribe in Paris. The dim noise of the day's *baguettes* being delivered to the cafés on the Boulevard des Capucines below did not disturb him. Nor did they wake his beautiful young wife.

He was just twenty-one, a tall young man with the slight stoop of someone who is a touch embarrassed to be 6′ 3″, but whose confident, almost arrogant clear-blue eyes seemed to belie his round baby face. His wife Isabel, whom everyone called Gypsy, lay asleep beside him, her black hair and perfect Latin American complexion framed by the white linen pillow-case. Although her eyes were closed, her cheeks seemed to glow with the joy that their first child was due within six weeks. They had been married barely four months.

At that moment Jimmy Goldsmith and Isabel Patino were the most publicly happy young couple in the world: the previous December they had eloped to Scotland, pursued not only by Isabel's exceptionally rich and angry father, Dom Antenor Patino, heir to a Bolivian tin fortune worth an estimated £75 million, but also by the world's press. After dodging their pursuers for a fortnight, and fighting off a court injunction, they had been secretly married in Kelso, Roxburghshire, a town once described by Sir Walter Scott as the most romantic in Scotland, on 7 January. Even the London *Daily Mirror*'s columnist Cassandra had admitted that their marriage was 'as romantic as a motorized version of Lorna Doone'. What none of the 130 journalists from around the world who pursued the young couple in those chilly January days knew was that young Isabel, who was still only eighteen, was already three months pregnant. Jimmy and Isabel had eloped because they were expecting a child.

13

But their marriage had clearly been a success. The small dark girl with the fierce eyes and determined spirit had been more than a match for the restless young man who had made his name at Eton by winning £8000 on the horses. They argued over everything, but always over nothing, and they were, according to their friends, 'transparently happy'. After the wedding Jimmy and Isabel returned to Paris, and while looking for an apartment they lived with his parents at the Hotel Scribe. His father, Major Frank Goldsmith, was chairman of the hotel and lived in a suite on the fourth floor with his wife when he was in Paris; Jimmy and Isabel lived in the suite directly above them.

That May was unusually hot for Paris, and the night before they had dined alone together on the terrace of a restaurant in Montmartre. The following morning, Jimmy did not bother to wake his wife before he set off across the Place de l'Opéra to his father's office in the Rue de la Paix for work. Nevertheless there was a whisper of concern in his mind. She seemed very tired, as though the pregnancy were preventing her from shrugging off sleep; and so when he got to the office he telephoned his mother to ask if she would go and see Isabel.

Well before ten o'clock Madame Goldsmith quietly let herself into the fifth-floor suite, crossed the oval sitting room and opened the bedroom door. Her daughter-in-law did not stir as she walked across to the bed and took her hand. It was quite limp.

Within an hour the still-unconscious eighteen-year-old had been transported across Paris to the Hartmann Clinic on the banks of the Seine at Neuilly, and an inconsolable Jimmy Goldsmith was desperately telephoning doctors around the world, bullying and cajoling them to come to Paris to treat his young wife. With a relentlessness that would become typical of him he paced the clinic's corridors, seizing anyone who might bring him news, before telephoning around the world again.

His efforts, though, were in vain. Three of France's most respected brain surgeons knew within minutes that Isabel Goldsmith had suffered a massive cerebral haemorrhage, and that their only hope of saving her was to trepan into her brain to relieve the pressure of the blood clot. That night they operated for the first time.

Still pacing the corridors outside, her young husband was told that it would take time to gauge the success of the operation. Isabel was moved into an oxygen tent and Jimmy waited. By the next day, Thursday, 13 May 1954, the doctors were warning him that they might not be able to save his wife; and there was the life of the child to be considered.

By Friday evening, no fewer than eleven eminent brain surgeons and gynaecologists, all assembled at the Hartmann Clinic, had reached the conclusion that the child had to be saved at once, and on the morning of Saturday, 15 May 1954, Jimmy and Isabel Goldsmith were delivered of a five-and-a-half pound baby daughter by Caesarian section.

Tragically, in spite of a further attempt to relieve the pressure on her brain, Maria Isabel Goldsmith died just before midnight, an hour after a priest had delivered the last rites. She never regained consciousness.

Jimmy Goldsmith walked out of the clinic into the darkness ignoring everyone. Perhaps he blamed himself for his young wife's death, for the doctors had told him that the haemorrhage had developed as a result of the pregnancy, and with them he had had to face the stark decision as to when the life-support systems should be withdrawn. From that day on, the man who was to become one of the world's most public tycoons lived every day as though it were his last.

1. Monsieur le Major

Perhaps Jimmy Goldsmith felt the fates were against him. Every Goldsmith for the past four hundred years had reason to feel this to some extent. For most of that time the family had lived in the Jewish ghetto in Frankfurt am Main in Germany, where barely twenty Jewish families had protected their businesses and themselves over the centuries by carefully intermarrying among themselves. A feeling of being an outsider was part of his birthright.

Yet being an outsider did no commercial harm. For just as in Florence in the fourteenth century so in Germany two hundred years later, the secular authorities prohibited banking and usury to Christians, and the Jews were imported to conduct financial affairs. The most celebrated banking dynasty in the world, the Rothschild family, started in the same Frankfurt ghetto, and indeed the Goldschmidts – as his family was then called – and the Rothschilds had intermarried. There are Goldschmidt-Rothschilds bankers in Frankfurt to this day, although the Goldschmidts always suspected they were the poorer cousins of the partnership. It was a suspicion that Jimmy Goldsmith would try to eradicate.

Nevertheless, as the nineteenth century drew to a close, at least some sections of the family felt their safety in the Frankfurt ghetto was no longer assured. The victory of the Prussians in 1866 convinced Jimmy Goldsmith's grandfather, Adolphus Goldschmidt, that he should leave.

One of fourteen brothers, Adolphus nevertheless brought with him to England a fortune estimated at more than £1 million, a charming manner, a small white goatee beard and, according to his sons, rather a twinkle in his eye. He also brought with him a wife, the respectable Miss Alice Merton from Birmingham, who was both attractive and suitable, her own father being a businessman of some substance in Germany.

With his wife and his considerable financial resources

Adolphus Goldschmidt set out to become an English country squire, and with this in mind bought a 5000-acre estate just west of the solid market town of Bury St Edmunds in Suffolk. The entire estate was known by the name of the small village at its heart, Cavenham, and its manor house was called Cavenham Hall. Adolphus invested his money in what he felt were the safest bonds he could find, those issued by the Czar of Russia and the Kaiser in Germany (the Goldschmidts had, after all, helped to raise finance for Bismarck). He even started a small bank with another cousin, but most of all he settled down to the life of shooting, hunting and fishing that befitted a squire in Victorian England.

In the meantime Alice Goldschmidt bore him four children, all of whom, however, were christened Goldsmith as a mark of respect for the family's newly adopted country. The first son, Charles, born in 1867, was followed by Edward in 1868, by a daughter, Nelly, and then, on 22 November 1878, by the youngest son, Frank. Mrs Goldschmidt raised her children to be more English than the English: no Yiddish was spoken at Cavenham Hall, indeed the only linguistic irregularity that sometimes punctuated the dinner-table conversation was the family dialect of Frankfurter Deutsch which had been refined in the ghetto. In every other respect Germany was put firmly behind them, and even fifty years later Frank Goldsmith never told his young sons that their grandfather had been born in Germany.

The three sons grew up handsome and charming but, with one exception, comparatively idle young men. Edward, who was known as Teddy, was always regarded as the best looking and the best shot; Charles was the best gambler, but Frank was the hardest working. Unlike his brothers, Frank was determined that he should have an education, and in pursuit of it set off to a crammers' in Cheltenham. By May 1897, at the age of eighteen, he had progressed well enough to take his Matriculation papers for Magdalen College, Oxford. He passed comfortably, taking some pleasure in answering a question on the 'use and abuse of the newspaper'.

With the fierceness of a man who wished to succeed,

18

Frank Goldsmith enjoyed Oxford. He graduated in 1900 with a good second in jurisprudence and the determination not only to study for his bar exams but also to pursue a career in politics. Life was not all examinations and ambitions, however, there were still the pastimes of a rich young Edwardian gentleman. The shooting parties with his cousins the Rothschilds and the Jessels, and the regular holidays in the South of France continued. After dinner the young men gambled at cards.

Frank's decision to go into politics did not surprise the Goldsmith family. They had enjoyed political connections since their arrival in England. Indeed by the time Frank Goldsmith reached Oxford the family's principal political friend and defender in England, Lord Rosebery, had become Prime Minister. Once again the connections from the Frankfurt ghetto sustained the family: Lord Rosebery had married a Rothschild.

Another cousin, Herbert Jessel, was already carving out a career for himself in the London County Council and on coming down from Oxford Frank Goldsmith followed his example. While still qualifying as a barrister – he was called to the bar at the Inner Temple in 1903 – he decided to stand as a Municipal Reform candidate for the Westminster City Council. The ambitious, Anglophile young man from Suffolk easily won the seat in the Council's Conduit ward, which included his flat in South Street, off Park Lane. It was November 1903, and he was not quite twenty-five.

Within a year he had added membership of the London County Council. In the autumn of 1904 he stood as a Municipal Reform candidate in the South St Pancras ward against the combined might of the two progressive candidates, one of whom was George Bernard Shaw, whose play *Caesar and Cleopatra* had only just come off in the West End. Undeterred by his renowned opponent, Frank Goldsmith won the seat comfortably, which provoked Shaw to remark tartly that 'beauty had beaten brains' in the election. Even *The Times* reported: ' "The best looking man gets my vote" was a remark frequently made by the women electors.'

To celebrate his success, and to indicate his determination to support King and Country, Frank Goldsmith also decided to join his local regiment, the Duke of York's Loyal Suffolk Hussars, the Suffolk Yeomanry. He was rewarded with a commission, and the horseback manoeuvres he took part in with his fellow officers became an adjunct of his weekends at Cavenham Hall.

During the week, however, he devoted himself energetically to London and the committees of both the Westminster City and London County Councils, taking particular interest in education. In 1907 Frank Goldsmith resigned his seat on Westminster's Council but not only retained his South St Pancras seat on the LCC, this time in partnership with one of the more celebrated actor-managers of the day, George Alexander, but also became a whip for the Municipal Reform Party at County Hall. It showed a determination that was shortly to bring him to the attention of the Conservative and Unionist Party.

In January 1910, when Asquith decided to go to the country over the delicate question of reform of the recalcitrant House of Lords, which was steadfastly blocking his Liberal Government's attempts to create the beginnings of a welfare state, Frank Goldsmith was offered the chance to fight a Parliamentary seat on behalf of the Conservatives. It was his home constituency of North West Suffolk, based at Stowmarket not far from Cavenham Hall.

After declaring in his election address that he was 'opposed to the payment of Members of Parliament', not to mention 'opposed to single-chamber government' and 'opposed to Home Rule' for Ireland (as indeed was Lord Rosebery), Frank Goldsmith won the seat from the Liberals by the decisive majority of 645 votes. At the age of thirty-one Frank Goldsmith had established the foundations of a political career which seemed destined to take him into a future Conservative Cabinet.

In December 1910, when Asquith called the second General Election of the year, Frank Goldsmith won again, although after a stiffer fight from his Liberal opponent his majority was reduced to 191. His unashamed Englishness, coupled with an ability to talk appealingly to crowds of any size and background, probably won him the day even more than the pledges contained in his election address. In only six years he had effortlessly climbed the heights of the Edwardian establishment. He was elected a Freemason, made a member of the Tattersall's committee at Newmarket and became a Justice of the Peace in Suffolk, as well as a county alderman. But he hardly had time to enjoy the fruits of his success before they were snatched away from him.

It is easy in retrospect to view the next four years in England as a tranquil interlude before the storm swept across Europe in 1914 – a time of innocent youth, of boaters and bustles – yet the reality was quite different. The troubles in Ireland were causing an uproar in the House of Commons. The suffragettes were threatening the basis of family life, and the new militancy of the trade unions was making a general strike a real possibility for the first time. Indeed, had it not been for the events in Sarajevo that summer, the general strike which had been called for 1914 would certainly have been as significant a part of English history as its counterpart twelve years later.

Throughout all this, Frank Goldsmith played his part in the country's political life. He was a young Tory on the rise. Likeable and articulate, his circle included Winston Churchill, Sir Edward Carson and another young rising politician, F. E. Smith, with whom he played cards at the St James's Club off Pall Mall. But the talk in smoking rooms in those four years was not just of politics. There was Dr Crippen's arrest aboard the SS *Montrose*, the tragic death of Captain Scott on his way back from the South Pole, Miss Emily Davison's suicide under the King's horse at the Derby and the disaster that struck closest to the heart of most wealthy families in Edwardian England, the sinking of the *Titanic*.

But just as he seemed to have settled into a life of powerful respectability, Captain Frank Goldsmith of the Suffolk Yeomanry, Conservative and Unionist MP for Stowmarket and Edwardian gentleman was drowned by the tide of anti-German feeling that swept across England. Hardly a decade before, the Germans had been regarded as hard-working and solid and, what is more, relatives of the English Royal Family. Yet within a matter of four years they were transformed in the public mind into military dullards manipulated by a histrionic Kaiser who was intent on creating a monstrous navy to dictate to the world.

Fanned by Lord Northcliffe's new *Daily Mail*, then the most popular paper in England, the first flickers of jingoism became a fire of public hysteria. Harmless old men who had forgotten to take out naturalization papers forty years earlier found themselves threatened with internment, bakers' shops with German-sounding names were looted, and, as A. J. P. Taylor has pointed out, even the new hard tennis courts in the grounds of country houses were dug up by suspicious locals who feared they might be used for gun emplacements by an invading German army.

Frank Goldsmith, who had been born in England, but whose father was still called Goldschmidt, did not escape.

No one could protect him against the tide of feeling that was running against all things German. Demands that he should be stripped of his commission were followed by rioting in his Stowmarket constituency. Bewildered, the young MP who prided himself on his Englishness found himself paying hospital bills for the men who had fought to defend him in the villages around his home.

In the clubs of London and in Parliament people whom he had regarded as his friends also turned against him; and although some remained loyal, notably Winston Churchill and Lord Bessborough (who helped him retain his commission in the Suffolk Yeomanry) there was no concealing the shock he felt. The convinced Anglophile, who had been determined to succeed at all things English, suddenly found himself an outsider again. The experience was to change his life.

For although he spent the next three years in active service with the Suffolk Yeomanry, first on the beaches at Gallipoli and then under Allenby in Palestine, seeing action at the two battles of Gaza, Frank Goldsmith never recovered from the feeling of rejection by a country which represented everything he held most dear. It was a humiliation that his son Jimmy was to remember. The English establishment would learn that the Goldsmiths were not to be so summarily rejected.

In November 1917 Frank Goldsmith, by then a Major,

quietly applied for leave to return from his army posting in Paris to his duties in the House of Commons. He took a brief trip to England to set his affairs in order and to tell his party that he did not intend to stand for reelection as an MP, and he returned to Paris. The following year, just as the war came to a close, his father died and Cavenham Hall was put up for sale. In December 1918 Frank Goldsmith saw his safe seat taken over by his old friend and fellow Yeomanry officer, Walter Guinness. The Liberal Party did not even bother to put up a candidate against him, so certain were they of losing.

Life in Paris had some advantages. France it may have been, but it was still the life of a gentleman. Even more significantly, Frank Goldsmith had fallen in love for the first time in his life with a young French girl called Jacqueline Franc. Although he was by no means enormously wealthy (his father's fortune had disappeared along with the Czar and the Kaiser), his mother had inherited a considerable sum which she used to support her son. But 'Monsieur le Major', as he soon became known in Paris, did not enjoy being idle. He bought some cinema shares, only to sell them in favour of shares in an hotel which allowed him to sustain the gentleman's life without paying for the servants that were necessary to maintain it. By accident he had stumbled upon a career which suited him admirably.

Within the next decade 'Monsieur le Major' established himself as the most successful and celebrated hotelier in Europe. In the sigh of relief that greeted the end of the war, Frank Goldsmith's effortless charm endeared him to the highest society of the times. No doubt his kinship with the Rothschilds helped, as did his former membership of the House of Commons, but it was his delight in the luxurious and his determination to see that his guests were well cared for that were decisive.

By 1928 Frank Goldsmith's Hotel Réunis chain controlled forty-eight of the best hotels in France including the Hotel Scribe and the Hotel Astoria in Paris, and the Carlton in Cannes. He also managed the principal hotels in Monte Carlo, including the Hotel de Paris and the

Hermitage, as well as the Café de Paris. The hotel business swept him around France and he moved from suite to suite wrapped in a magnificent fur-collared coat like an elegant nomad.

From the Scribe in the spring and autumn he would travel on to the Carlton in the winter for the season on the Côte d'Azur and then perhaps on to London to see his brothers, while staying in a suite at Claridges. Indeed, before the 1920s were over, the Savoy Company invited him to become a director of its group of hotels which included the Savoy, the Berkeley and Claridges.

In the heady days of the early 1920s 'Monsieur le Major' travelled with no small pomp and no little circumstance. His cases were always carried by a string of porters, out of the hotel to the waiting car and from there on to the waiting train and its first class compartment. He took delight in bringing the foyers of his hotels to a momentary halt with the sheer size of his entourage. For although not a particularly vain man just under six feet tall, he took pride in his sense of style, and pleasure in the opulence his hotels allowed him.

He never talked about the political career he might have enjoyed, nor indeed about his life in England, although he had been awarded an OBE in 1921; he preferred instead to live his life to the full in France, rootless but comfortably luxurious.

He and Jacqueline tried to start a family together, but without success. In desperation she decided to have an operation to unblock her fallopian tubes, which had been diagnosed as the cause of their difficulties. In a strange harbinger of the experience that was to overtake his son more than thirty years later, she died after the operation, leaving 'Monsieur le Major' heartbroken.

After Jacqueline's death there were a number of lady companions, some of them married, some not; but it was on a trip to Cannes in the company of one of the married ladies that Frank Goldsmith found part of the solidity that he was searching for. His travelling companion was to stay with her mother and younger sister at the family's villa in Cannes, and she was to be entertained while she was there by the slightly balding but well groomed hotelier with the twinkle in his eye. He had come to oversee the necessary alterations at the Carlton in preparation for the winter season, and to look into his hotels at Monte Carlo. When the couple descended from the Blue Train they were met by the lady's younger sister, a striking blonde girl with blue eyes called Marcelle Mouillier. Their father had run hotels in their native Vichy, where he was a socialist member of the municipal council. The following day she escorted the couple to Monte Carlo for lunch, even though she was too young at eighteen to join them in the Casino afterwards.

When her sister's week in Cannes was over, the young blonde girl accompanied 'Monsieur le Major' and her sister to the station, partly because she wanted to see inside the famous Blue Train. While she was examining the panelled sitting rooms and hand-made beds, the train slipped quietly out of the station. Marcelle Mouillier was not in the least dismayed. Even though she was wearing only a light summer dress over her swimming costume, and had no luggage, she was determined not to be put off at the first available stop. For an adventurous young girl who had never been to Paris it was a perfect opportunity.

In Paris she stayed demurely with her sister, content to be entertained by the charming Major who seemed to know everyone at all the best places. There were visits to Ciros and the Ritz, which might have overwhelmed an ordinary eighteen-year-old who had hardly ventured more than 100 kilometres from Vichy, but they did not. She possessed a fierceness of spirit and a pride which quite captivated the Major.

Within a year 'Monsieur le Major', by now a Chevalier de la Légion d'Honneur, and the young girl from the Auvergne were more than friends, and in June 1927, shortly after the birth of their first child, they married quietly in London during one of the Major's business trips. At the age of forty-eight the most celebrated hotelier in Europe had taken a wife who was not old enough to enter the casinos in the hotels he ran.

After their son Edward, named after his uncle and always called Teddy by the family, was born in a clinic in Paris, the Major decided that the family needed a home more permanent than a series of hotel suites. So when Marcelle returned home it was not to his suite at the Scribe but to an apartment a short pram's-push from the Bois de Boulogne. Although it was not particularly prepossessing from the outside, the apartment at 43 Rue Emile Menier was in the suitably fashionable 16 ième arrondissement and was large enough to accommodate the staff that Frank Goldsmith believed his new family needed. A nurse and a cook were hired, as was a maid, and later a governess. He would travel back from his office in the Rue de la Paix in his Rolls Royce, which naturally had its own chauffeur.

It was into this magnificently cossetted life that on 26 February 1933 a second son was born to Major Frank and Madame Marcelle Goldsmith. They called him James Michael.

2. The Sporting Life

It was a gilded childhood. The unquestioned affluence of Jimmy Goldsmith's early years left him oblivious to the possibility that life could be lived in any other way. Dinner was always a matter of white tie and tails, parties were always extravagant and peopled by the most celebrated figures of the day, the girls were usually pretty and yet sometimes bored.

It was the time of *Private Lives*, when Noel Coward and Gertrude Lawrence played out their stuttering romance on the balcony of a hotel on the Riviera which could well have been owned and managed by 'Monsieur le Major' Frank Goldsmith. Together with his mother and father, not to mention his brother Teddy and their considerable staff, Jimmy Goldsmith spent his first six years living in the grandest hotel suites of Europe, welcome in every city from Paris to Biarritz, from the Alps to the Côte d'Azur. He was a small boy for whom the terrace of the Carlton in Cannes or the first-floor suites of Claridges in London were as commonplace as a suburban garden. The memory of those first six years, and the taste for opulence they gave him has never left him; nor, perhaps, has the impression that any small boy would have gathered in those glittering circumstances – that life is as much about play as work. Little hint of the depression or of the turmoil that was beginning to grip Europe penetrated his fairy-tale world.

It was not the same society, however, that Major Frank Goldsmith had known as a boy. The gaiety was more forced, the attitudes more brittle than the confident days before the war; and, more significantly, as the *Tatler* commented, 'during the first ten years after the war came a social revolution that upset all preconceived ideas of Society. Birth became of less importance than riches'. Nothing could have suited 'Monsieur le Major' and his family better, for along with that social change had come

27

acceptance of the tribes of the Frankfurt ghetto as welcome members of Society, and the Goldsmiths were well connected. Lionel Rothschild had been the first Jew to be elevated to the peerage, and one of James Michael Goldsmith's godfathers was the Baron James de Rothschild. Although no particular emphasis was placed on religion by the boy's governess, nor indeed by his father, the family tradition was not forgotten, no matter how little it was discussed.

It was also an upbringing that bred a self-assurance that could seem like arrogance. Everything was always provided; there was never any suggestion that anything would ever be withheld. The small boy who had inherited his mother's fiercely blue eyes, and his father's wide, boyish face accepted his birthright without hesitation, although he added to it a sometimes volcanic impatience that would in the end become the despair of even his parents.

Spring was spent in Paris, with a trip on to London for a few weeks, then it was on to the south of France, before returning to Paris en route to the Alps. Even this opulent lifestyle may become boring if you have known nothing else. To those born to it, there is the demand for a little excitement, and Jimmy Goldsmith took his in gambling.

The attractions of cards had always played their part in the family life. His father still played regularly at the St James's Club in London and the Travellers' in Paris, although roulette had its devotees among his brothers. Jimmy Goldsmith's uncle Charles had long been a regular visitor to the fashionable casino at Ostend, so regular in fact that when he began to lose persistently he became convinced that his misfortunes were due to the subtle influence of the King of the Belgians (a claim for which there was not the slightest justification). Uncle Charles ended his days quietly in a house in the grounds of a Swiss sanatorium with his wife, when the excitement of the roulette wheel grew too much for him.

Even at the age of six, however, Jimmy Goldsmith was fascinated by the prospect of a profit from chance. One morning in the early summer of 1939 he stood watching an elderly American lady struggling to make the primitive gambling machine in the drawing room of the Carlton Hotel pay a small return for her steady supply of one-franc pieces. Finally the lady gave up her attempt to extract a prize from the machine and left the room. Within a matter of seconds the small boy, a determined look on his face, climbed on to a chair and pressed his own one-franc piece into the slot. He pulled the handle, and in a matter of seconds found himself standing in a puddle of coins so large that it took two waiters to collect them all. Jimmy Goldsmith had won the jackpot.

Without a moment's hesitation he directed two waiters to collect his winnings and to follow him. He was off in search of his mother. In fact Madame Goldsmith had already seen her son's triumph, and had told his father. Spotting his parents bearing down on him, he grabbed his winnings, by then on a silver platter, and took off across the Carlton Hotel's foyer towards the lift, pursued by his parents. Clearly dismayed at the thought they might confiscate his winnings, he rushed into the lift, operated the manual handle himself and set off towards the family suite. His parents ran up the stairs after him. As he reached the suite, however, so his parents arrived and, again without hesitating, Jimmy Goldsmith rushed back into the lift and disappeared downwards. Even at six he was not to have his independence threatened or to be separated from his winnings.

The Côte d'Azur gave Jimmy Goldsmith his sense of the style in which life should be lived. These were the years when girls were still sent to £120-a-term finishing schools in Paris to learn bridge, and 'do' a cathedral and a museum a week, while their parents made sure they spent at least part of the year in Monte Carlo or Cannes. They were only following the example, after all, of the future King of England, for in 1935 the Prince of Wales stayed at the Carlton and was looked after by 'Monsieur le Major' with his customary charm, just as another guest at the same time, Mrs Wallis Simpson, was looked after with equal care by his wife.

Although the *Tatler* reported on 6 September 1939 the crisis 'robbed Deauville of many of its most regular supporters before Grand Prix Days', it went on to add, 'there was still a good attendance for a very exciting day's racing'. The rumblings of war had certainly hardly perturbed the community in Cannes. It was to be some weeks before the possibility of a holocaust struck Major Frank Goldsmith forcefully. He may have been one of the most prominent hoteliers in France, and a Jew, although not a particularly devout one, but like thousands of others he had believed another war with Germany was unthinkable.

Realizing the danger, and aware that the French army was not likely to prove a particularly adequate defence, 'Monsieur le Major' despatched his wife and sons from the comfort of the Carlton. He had heard that the best hope of a safe return to England was to catch a boat from Bayonne on France's south-west coast. The journey to the Atlantic from the Mediterranean took Madame Goldsmith and her sons two days, and when they arrived they had to wait longer for the Major than they had envisaged. Indeed, by the time he arrived – inevitably driven in his Rolls Royce – the town was swarming with people with very much the same idea of escape. Undeterred, Madame Goldsmith took her place on the quayside to wait, ignoring the rumours circulating that no boats were coming, that the harbour was about to be bombed or that the Germans had blockaded the port so that as soon as anyone put to sea they would be killed. She waited three days; while her son Jimmy became the only one of the family who seemed to have the knack of finding food among the tumult in the town.

On the third day a Dutch freighter slipped into the mouth of the Adour river and embarked as many passengers as it could carry for a voyage back to England. It was to be the last ship to escape from Bayonne, and the Goldsmith family climbed gratefully on board, even though they had to sleep on the deck. Another of the passengers was their cousin Evelyn Rothschild. Even then the danger was not quite passed: in the Bay of Biscay a marauding U-boat fired a single torpedo at the freighter, but it slipped harmlessly past.

Once in England, however, conditions for the Goldsmiths reverted to the comfort of Cannes, even though war had been declared. 'Monsieur le Major' and his family settled themselves gratefully in a suite at Claridges, although within a matter of hours of their arrival they were forced to retire to the hotel's cellars as the sirens sounded for an air raid. Nevertheless they were to stay happily in the hotel for some months before it was decided that the possibility of a blitz, or an invasion, dictated that the boys should be evacuated. As the Major's request to be taken into the services again had been turned down on the grounds that he was sixty-one, he decided the family should go together and in the early summer of 1940, before the skies over Kent filled with dogfights, Frank Goldsmith and his family set out by boat from beneath the barrage balloons over Liverpool for the rather less austere surroundings of the Bahamas.

The next four years were peaceful enough for the Major and his family. He occupied himself working at the Royal Victoria Hotel in Nassau, where they stayed – causing his sons to remark to each other, 'it was the first time in his life he had actually worked for somebody else' – while Madame Goldsmith helped to run a canteen for trainee air force pilots organized by the Duchess of Windsor, who had arrived on the Caribbean island shortly after the Goldsmiths: the wife of the colony's new governor. When she spotted her friends at the first official reception the Duchess could hardly contain her glee at finding a face she knew.

So the familiar round of parties, dinners and conversation, punctuated by gentle afternoons of rest away from the heat of the tropical sun, returned for 'Monsieur le Major' and his wife. For their sons, however, life was a little different from the South of France. They were now supposed to be furthering their education, and there was the Belmont School on the island to be attended.

Jimmy Goldsmith was not impressed by the need to extend his academic horizons. He preferred games of chance where he could find them, particularly the American dice game of 'craps'. During the next three years he tended to greet the attempts to force him to do things he did not care for with a display of his formidable temper. But though some might have called him a spoilt child, others would later remember only his considerable charm. 'He was the most remarkable little boy,' one of his father's contemporaries recalls. 'It was as if he wasn't a child at all, just a slightly smaller adult, he conducted himself so seriously and in such an unchildlike way.'

By the time he was nine, however, Jimmy Goldsmith's father had decided that his lack of interest in schooling demanded some serious attention. Together with his brother Teddy he was despatched to St Andrew's College near Toronto in Canada so that his education might be taken rather more seriously in hand. The Major clearly felt that the chillier atmosphere of Canada might induce a touch more discipline than the relaxed climate on a tropical island.

It would not be the only time, however, that an attempt to turn Jimmy Goldsmith into a serious student proved a failure. But it was not only academic work that he took exception to, he also did not care for any kind of sport. In the deliberately athletic surroundings of a school trying to ape the traditions of an English public school it was an attitude which did not make him popular.

Jimmy Goldsmith refused to co-operate with any effort to make him a sportsman, no matter how fierce the punishments threatened in reprisal. Indeed there was no more precise example of his studied rebellion than the school's annual cross-country race.

Every boy was expected to take part, and the course was designed to end in the school's quadrangle, where the runners were to be greeted by staff and parents with an appropriate cheer. As the race got under way it became abundantly clear that James Michael Goldsmith was a none-too-enthusiastic competitor. After an hour or more every boy in the school had completed the course, running into the quadrangle to suitable encouragement from family and friends; except, that is, for Jimmy Goldsmith. Some fifteen minutes after the last boy had finished the course the tallish ten-year-old strolled into the quadrangle, studiously walking rather than running. He was carrying a bag of toffees in one hand and a copy of the *Toronto Sporting Chronicle* in the other. Perusing the racing pages, Jimmy Goldsmith ostentatiously completed the course in a deafening silence. It was the action of a boy who regarded himself as apart from the crowd, someone who would never hesitate to draw attention to himself no matter what ridicule he might attract by doing so. He might finish last but everyone would remember how he did it.

By the end of 1944 the Goldsmiths decided to send their sons back to England in search of an education. The Major was anxious that at least one of his sons should go to his old college at Oxford. So it was arranged that the boys should go to Millfield School in Somerset, then under the control of the formidable R. J. O ('Boss') Meyer; Teddy to be crammed for Oxford, Jimmy to be prepared for the common entrance and Eton. While the boys were on the boat they heard that Franklin Roosevelt had died, to be succeeded as President by Harry Truman.

By now distinctly tall for his age, but still with his father's open face, Jimmy Goldsmith had at least one significant advantage when he arrived at Millfield. He could speak French. His mother had addressed him and his brother in little else throughout their childhood, partly because she had known hardly any English when she had first travelled to London to marry the Major, and partly because she was determined the two boys should speak the two languages of their dual nationality. For although both her sons had been born in France they were also entitled to British citizenship because of their English father. 'Monsieur le Major', on the other hand, had always addressed his sons in English. He was, after all, still an English gentleman at heart and proud of it, a man keen to see his son go to Eton, even though no other member of the family had ever been there.

Jimmy Goldsmith was not in the slightest deterred by Millfield or its stern headmaster. If anything, he took some pleasure, as he was for many years to come, in outwitting the school authorities in pursuit of his love of gambling. Bets were placed by postal order and delivered by other boys in defiance of the school rules. Nonetheless, the efforts of the Millfield staff were to some effect, for in 1946 Jimmy passed into Eton and in October 1947 – exactly fifty years after his father – Teddy went up to Magdalen College, Oxford, as an undergraduate.

Opportunities for enjoyment at Eton soon presented

themselves. He contrived to ignore most classes, and determinedly refused to take part in sports. Instead, he proceeded to throw dinner parties for his friends in Windsor and take parties to the races there whenever possible. His allowance of £1 a week from 'Monsieur le Major', who had by then returned to France to take up the reigns of his hotel chain again, was clearly not anywhere near enough to sustain the lifestyle he was leading, but that never appeared to give Jimmy Goldsmith the slightest anxiety. Money for him then, and indeed from then onwards, did not assume the same significance as it did for those from more humdrum homes. He always assumed, as he told his friends, that if things got too difficult his father would pay.

The next three years were not passed in the cloistered calm that is usually associated with Britain's most celebrated public school. For although Jimmy Goldsmith accepted that he might not exactly fit the nineteenth-century conception of a member of the English establishment, he could still use his wits and his financial acumen to make life there as enjoyable as possible. In almost every way he succeeded. Instead of being treated as an outsider Jimmy Goldsmith resolutely formed his own collection of friends, whom he later described as 'misfits, eccentrics or rebels' because 'I was a bit foreign and not good at games.' Although not times of enormous academic achievement – he did not pass a single examination to anyone's knowledge – the days at Eton were significant to the development of the legend of Jimmy Goldsmith. Indeed at least one of his most prominent adversaries in his later life, Richard Ingrams, the editor of *Private Eye*, believed for a time that the explanation of his personality could be traced back solely to his time at the school, and to the reasons for his leaving suddenly at the age of sixteen.

In the years since he left, legend after legend has built up about Jimmy Goldsmith's departure from Eton. His enemies have maintained he was expelled. 'There has always been some doubt about whether I was sacked or not from Eton,' he said later. 'Fortunately this doubt can be put to rest. There is a tradition that a boy leaving Eton without being sacked is given a book by the headmaster in a little "going down ceremony", and I still have the book I was given in Paris, suitably inscribed. However I was no success at Eton.'

His departure took place shortly after a remarkable win at Lewes races: Jimmy Goldsmith won £8000 on a three-horse accumulator. He can recall the names of the three horses, Bartisan, Merry Dance and Your Fancy, and more than twenty years afterwards John Aspinall, who had been at Rugby, gave him a present of a solid gold box engraved with the names of his companies throughout the world. Inside the box there was a simpler engraving – it bore the names of the three horses in the bet. After his win he took almost his entire house at Eton out to lunch. A contemporary at Eton, Digby Neave, recalls now, 'It wasn't the sort of thing you did, but Jimmy went ahead and did it.' He said himself later, 'I did not believe a man of such means should still be at school.'

But that successful £1 bet was by no means the only bet Jimmy Goldsmith made during his time at Eton. It was simply one of hundreds, some successful, some not, which, coupled with his apparent disregard for the traditions and attitudes at the school, had continued to convince at least some of the staff that perhaps he was not benefitting greatly from what Eton had to offer. He was so determined to succeed that he avoided anything he thought he might be less than good at, like games. At the same time his parents were growing increasingly concerned as reports of his more outrageous behaviour filtered back to them in France.

Like all rebels, however, although he rejected the established order, he also depended upon it as a point of reference for his rebellion. He was always anxious, for example, that his mother should never wear too outrageous a hat when she came down to see him. His parents finally agreed with him and the school that he might be happier in rather less formal surroundings.

So, shortly after his magnificently flamboyant gesture of treating his house to lunch on the strength of his £8000 winnings, Jimmy Goldsmith left Eton for the less precise disciplines of a crammer's in Kent. But he did not go straight there. Instead he went to Oxford to visit his brother Teddy, by then in his final year at Magdalen, and that night got involved in a *chemin de fer* game with his brother. Within hours of arriving at Oxford, Goldsmith was plunged into the regular game that took place either at Teddy's room in Magdalen, or more often at John Aspinall's digs at 167 Walton Street. By the end of the evening Jimmy had lost a considerable proportion of his winnings, because he had not realized that all the other members of the game were playing primarily with IOUs while he was playing with real money.

The freedom of Walton Street and the eccentricity it allowed him, meant that he returned to Oxford regularly over the next few months. His occasional tenure at the crammer's came to an end when his temper broke through one day and a fight started with one of the masters. Afterwards, Goldsmith felt it prudent to withdraw. His was the temper of a boy who had never wholly accepted the right of anyone to control him.

Digby Neave remembers that he 'may only have been seventeen but he seemed older than anyone else of his age', and in an Oxford rooming house Jimmy Goldsmith found a way of life that suited him. After the rigours of school there was now nothing reprehensible in indolence, providing it was entertaining and was paid for by somebody else. 'Jimmy had an electrifying effect on the place,' Neave recalls. 'Things really began to happen.'

Among the things that began to happen was that Jimmy Goldsmith discovered one of the passions that would never leave him, the company of beautiful women. One of the many visitors to 167 Walton Street was a girl who occasionally wore around the house an elaborate silk dressing gown tied at the waist which nevertheless had small holes cut in it so that her nipples showed through. He remembers it to this day.

So, free from the pressures of Eton and the crammers, Goldsmith settled contentedly into life at Oxford, devoting himself to as entertaining a life as possible, punctuating it with poker, parties and pretty girls. At one of the poker games Teddy and Digby Neave competed with each other over a particular hand. Teddy lost. 'He said he couldn't pay the £40 he owed me,' Neave remembers, 'but I could have Jimmy's car instead. It was a 1928 Singer and still at the crammer's, so I went off to get it. We drove around Oxford in it for years until it finally fell to pieces.'

The idyll did not last, however, for Jimmy's father began to receive worrying reports of his son's activities in Oxford. By the middle of 1950, when Jimmy Goldsmith was just seventeen, relations between 'Monsieur le Major' and his younger son were becoming distinctly strained, even though Jimmy had by then returned to Paris where he was working as a cook and waiter at the Luce Restaurant in Montmartre. His father decided that his wayward son, who seemed to have no intention of doing anything much beyond enjoying himself, should take up a career; and the obvious choice was the hotel business. To learn the trade, 'Monsieur le Major' decided to despatch his son to the Palace Hotel in Madrid, a haunt of Ernest Hemingway. Jimmy Goldsmith was to start as a member of the *hors d'oeuvre* department in the hotel kitchens.

Once again the Major's plans for his son did not go precisely to plan. Undismayed, Jimmy Goldsmith set himself up in a splendid apartment near the Prado, only a short walk along the Plaza de las Cortes from the 600-roomed hotel, and invited his friends to stay with him. Calling on the many former employees of his father's hotels throughout Europe for help, he proceeded to create for himself a life not all that different from the one he had left at Oxford, although perhaps on a rather grander scale.

One place it was not conducted from was the *hors d'oeuvre* department of the Palace Hotel.

When news came of his son's failure to stick to the career he had chosen for him, 'Monsieur le Major' telephoned and instructed him to go to the hotel at once. He went, only to return home with a large quantity of caviar which had originally been intended for a reception for President Franco.

But before long even that sojourn, punctuated as ever with gambling, although on *pelota* rather than cards, came to an end. Major Goldsmith was beginning to realize that his son was out of control, and more particularly he was being asked to settle some £2000 of his son's debts. Digby

Neave was despatched to the Berkeley Hotel to sort matters out. 'I think I was regarded as the serious friend. I was trotted out to talk to Jimmy's parents.'

The sorting out was duly done, but at a price. Major Goldsmith had decided that he would settle his son's debts only if he volunteered for the army. So Neave took the somewhat disconsolate Goldsmith to Victoria to sign on for his national service rather earlier than he had intended.

Partly at his father's insistence, Jimmy Goldsmith opted for a regiment which was stationed a very considerable distance from the temptations of London. He chose the Royal Artillery, and began his training at Oswestry, finally becoming a training officer for the difficult young men with whom the Royal Artillery did not quite know how to cope. It proved a classic piece of man-management by the army: the poacher was turned gamekeeper. Lieutenant Goldsmith ruled his recalcitrant youths with as stern a rod as any there had ever been. For a young man who had not been exactly unfamiliar with assaulting his own masters at school, both in Canada and in England, the task of keeping a platoon from assaulting him proved instructive. He was to claim later that the army 'made a man of me'. In the meantime he was sustaining himself with an affair with a contortionist who worked at a holiday camp.

3. Flight to Casablanca

Life in the Royal Artillery did not put an end to Jimmy
Goldsmith's rich and studiedly eccentric lifestyle, but it
did teach him the virtue of occasionally curbing the flam-
boyance he had taken for granted since he was a child. He
may have despised the reticence of the average member of
the English upper classes, but he came to realize in the
army that in order to survive he had to accept their desire
for composure in public, no matter how licentious they
chose to be in private. It was an ambivalence he would
always find difficult to accept.

But even more significantly, by the first months of 1953
when he completed his premature national service – which
had saved him from becoming a fireman in Melbourne,
Australia, as one of his father's lawyers had seriously
recommended – Jimmy Goldsmith had realized that he had
to have something to do. The experience of his platoon
of potential borstal boys had given him the taste for a sense
of direction in life.

His friends from Oxford had already begun to settle into
their careers, as many of them had done their own national
service before going up to the university, and so rather than
limp idly round London, gathering debts and repeating
the mistakes of two years earlier, Jimmy Goldsmith returned to France. 'Monsieur le Major' welcomed him back,
and provided a small room on the seventh floor of the
Hotel Scribe, in what were once the servants' quarters.
There remained the delicate question, however, of what his
son should do for a living.

Jimmy Goldsmith was to find his career in the most
unlikely place. Rather as his father had stumbled into the
hotel business on coming out of the Army in 1918, so his
son stumbled into the pharmaceutical industry because his
brother Teddy happened to meet a man on an aeroplane. Meeting people on all forms of public transport was
one of the family's habits, and on this occasion Teddy had

met a Dr William Moss, the inventor of Lloyd's Adrenalin Cream which, he claimed, alleviated the worst effects of rheumatism.

Teddy Goldsmith, who had already started as an entrepreneur in a small but rather unsuccessful way with a firm to make electrical plugs, persuaded Dr Moss that he should set up a company to represent and distribute his cream in France. And after an exercise in public-relations, in which the cream was rubbed into the painful joints of a horse destined to take part in the Prix de l'Arc de Triomphe – it managed to come third after the application – Teddy Goldsmith had forged ahead.

Before he could get his pharmaceutical company properly under way, however, Teddy was arrested for failing to report for his French national service. It was a mistake, the call-up papers had never reached him, but the experience prompted him to decide that the time had probably come to do his national service somewhere. He opted for Britain. So in the early summer of 1953 Teddy Goldsmith handed over his company, which he had named Dagonal after the god of crop fertility known in Palestine as the god of the Philistines, to his brother Jimmy and left for England. From this unlikely beginning Jimmy Goldsmith was to fashion an empire.

Although he may not have precisely formulated the idea in his mind in those first weeks, he was to say later, 'I wanted to revive the family fortunes. I don't think my father could read a balance sheet until the end of his life. He ran his business in a very civilized way, but he was an amateur.' There was nothing that Jimmy Goldsmith liked to be less than to be an amateur. Even gambling he had approached with a determination born of an obsession to be good at it, a ruthless dedication to learn its intricacies and put them to work for his own benefit.

But hard though Jimmy worked to expand his brother's tiny business (Teddy had left him only one employee), it was not his commercial acumen that was to transform him from a virtually unknown young man into a public figure within a year.

It was an affair of the heart that was to put him on the front pages of virtually every newspaper in Europe and many in America, and he certainly did not plan it that way. Jimmy Goldsmith may have developed, in a very short time, a considerable appetite for the companionship of beautiful young women but he could not have known it was to alter his life. But then playboys, if they are true to their name, do not fall in love.

To the untutored eye Senor Dom Antenor Patino looked every inch a Bolivian nobleman. He conducted himself impeccably, he had been Bolivia's Ambassador to London during the war, and he had inherited a fortune estimated to be more than £75 million. What few people knew was that Senor Patino's own father, who had discovered and exploited a tin mine, was in fact an ambitious Red Indian who had skilfully created a fortune for both himself and his family. No matter how it may have appeared on the surface, Senor Patino's ancestry was one of ambition.

Nevertheless Senor Patino was determined that his two daughters, born to him by the niece of King Alfonso of Spain, Christina, the Duchess de Durcal, should have a proper station in life. With this in mind, he had brought them both to Paris so that they might meet young men of suitable position and wealth.

Christina and Maria Isabel Patino were blessed with spectacular beauty. They were both dark-skinned and dark-eyed, with a vivacity that seemed bred in a carnival, yet they shared an ability to become tranquil and serene in the company of their friends. With the benefit of an American education, and the finishing touches of sophistication of a Paris that was just welcoming the 'new look' in fashion, they caused a considerable stir. To their father's obvious delight a number of potentially acceptable suitors appeared. Indeed, before they had been in France very long, Senor Patino's elder daughter Christina had settled on marrying Prince Marc de Beauvau-Craon, whose family had a château near Nancy.

Senor Patino's younger daughter Isabel, however, presented more of a problem for her father. He had always accepted that she was the more headstrong of his daughters, but he had not counted on her dislike for quite so many of the titled young men he contrived to steer in her direction. For her part, Isabel Patino was none too keen on her father's ambitions for her, and she confided her doubts to Teddy Goldsmith, who in turn introduced her to his brother. They met during the early months of 1953 while Isabel was still flirting with a number of potential suitors, but the girl whom everyone always called Gypsy, partly because of her looks and her occasionally dramatic temper, was still fighting off any plans her father had for her future. She would make those herself.

Yet it was not until the night of her seventeenth birthday party in June that Isabel Patino realized that Jimmy Goldsmith might become a more serious suitor than any whom her father had in mind for her. That night Senor Patino had decided to give his daughter a party at his favourite London hotel, Claridges. Teddy Goldsmith and his wife Gill were invited and afterwards a small group, including the Goldsmiths, went on to the Casanova Club in Mayfair where they were joined by Teddy's younger brother Jimmy. It would not be the only time in Jimmy Goldsmith's life that a serious affair had begun in a Mayfair nightclub.

Jimmy Goldsmith had met rich and beautiful girls before. But there was something more to Isabel Patino than to the other little rich girls in Jimmy Goldsmith's life. She had a temperament to match his own. She was every bit as determined, every jot as fiery as he; and, what is more, she saw no reason why she should allow herself to be dominated by him. It was a strength he found hypnotizing. That evening, in the midst of the celebrations that swept London in the days before the Coronation of Queen Elizabeth II, Jimmy Goldsmith and Isabel Patino began to fall in love.

Over the next few weeks their attraction for each other deepened. Both had returned to Paris, she to pursue the social diary her father had arranged for her, he to run his tiny but expanding pharmaceutical company, which he had now called Laboratories Cassene, from his long-suffering father's offices in the Rue de la Paix. Throughout the summer they met regularly, until it became abundantly clear that, no matter how fervently her father may have hoped for a son-in-law with noble blood, his daughter was set upon a young man with a mixture of the Frankfurt ghetto and the Auvergne in his veins.

By the autumn Jimmy Goldsmith and Isabel Patino were lovers, and although Senor Patino may not have known that fact, he certainly feared that his daughter was becoming rather too close to the flamboyant young man whom his friends told him had something of a reputation as a gambler and a playboy.

It was only a matter of weeks before matters came to a head. Isabel Patino discovered she was pregnant, and Jimmy Goldsmith immediately decided to marry her, for, as he was to tell me much later, 'For me marriage is having a child, not signing a piece of paper.' Senor Patino was unmoved. He told the young man, 'We come from an old Catholic family,' to which he received the reply, 'Perfect, we come from an old Jewish family.' Enraged, Senor Patino went on, 'But it is not our habit to marry Jews.' Jimmy Goldsmith replied tartly, 'It is not our habit to marry Red Indians.' Senor Patino did not hesitate. He despatched his daughter and a chaperone on a tour of North Africa, beginning in Casablanca.

When Jimmy Goldsmith heard Isabel had gone, he was indignant. What was wrong with the Goldsmith family? Were they not respectable? Why should anyone view them as anything less than acceptable members of their family? In a matter of hours he had decided not only to follow Isabel but also to take her to Scotland and marry her. After hasty consultation with his lawyers he had discovered that it was possible to marry in Scotland without their parents' consent, and he was determined that his first child should be born to Mr and Mrs James Michael Goldsmith.

But he was also in a panic. Afraid that Dom Antenor might lock up his daughter in a convent for three years, or worse, in the words of one of his friends, he went 'slightly mad'. No sooner had Isabel Patino and her chaperone set off for Casablanca than Goldsmith was chartering a plane in Paris to follow her. A struggling businessman he might be, but in an affair of the heart he was not to be outdone by anyone – tin millionaire or not.

Together with his Eton contemporary Digby Neave, whom he had by then encouraged to come to Paris and start up in the insurance business, and another friend, John Train, he took off from Le Bourget to 'rescue Isabel' from the fate he imagined her father had in store for her. It was an adventure worthy of Hollywood, with its mixture of publicity, passion and the law. Although he may not have admitted it to himself at the time, it satisfied his passion for the dramatic, and his determination never to be dismissed as simply one of the crowd.

Unknown to Jimmy Goldsmith, however, just as his chartered de Havilland Dart took off from Le Bourget, Isabel Patino was landing at the same airport. Dom Antenor had got wind of the flight to rescue her and had ordered her home, so that he could personally supervise her future. Perhaps he even allowed himself a smile at the thought of his arrogant young adversary flying off in pursuit of someone he could have met by walking merely a few hundred yards.

To the anxious suitor, the flight to Casablanca seemed to take an eternity. The pilot had to refuel at Madrid, and by the time they had reached Moroccan port, the crew were so tired they had to go to bed. He, however, immediately started telephoning around Europe to discover where she had gone to, and it was then he discovered Senor Patino's plan. More incensed than ever, he decided to pursue his original intention: to arrange for their elopement to Scotland.

Using his secretary in Paris as his accomplice and with the help of a number of his friends, he arranged for Isabel's passport to be collected from her parents (hardly an easy task in the circumstances) and for her to be taken to Orly and put on a plane for London – all while he was still in Casablanca. He would meet her there by flying directly from Morocco. Though she lacked an exit visa from France, which she then needed as a Bolivian citizen, Isabel Patino still managed to slip out of France and on to England before her father noticed. She was met at Heathrow by another friend the *Daily Mirror* journalist Noel Whitcomb, at whose home Isabel was to stay.

Meanwhile, Jimmy Goldsmith plunged on with his planned elopement, by now aware that the world's press were beginning to take an interest. The *Daily Mirror* called the story when it finally broke, 'The Runaway heiress and the Playboy'. So when he finally reached

London after a stopover to refuel in Jersey and more telephone calls, Jimmy and Isabel were not only united, they were also placed in the back of a Rolls Royce provided by the *Daily Mirror* and despatched towards Scotland with a posse of journalists on their heels.

It was just before Christmas 1953, and the couple's romantic flight delighted the headline writers of every newspaper in Britain. The journey of the young gambler and the heiress who stood to inherit at least £2 million, bred an interest in an elopement not seen in Britain since Jessica Mitford had decided to escape her family's clutches before the war. Sightings were reported from up and down the country, hotel keepers were badgered, ports watched, and yet miraculously they were never found. In fact, on the way north from London they had done a perfectly obvious thing: they had stopped off to see Teddy Goldsmith at his officers' training camp near Chester; but even then the pursuing journalists did not catch up with them.

By the time they reached Edinburgh a few days before Christmas, the story of their elopement had become news throughout the world. Its implications had not been lost on Antenor Patino, who was by now under siege from inquiring newspapermen anxious to know what he planned to do about his daughter's disappearance. Senor Patino now saw his honour being drawn into question. No matter how loudly the newspapers might trumpet the 'true love' of the young couple, his daughter was still under age, and she remained his responsibility. He was not to be made to look a fool.

Antenor Patino decided, therefore, to set off for Edinburgh in search of his daughter, who by this time was living quietly at the home of a friend of her future husband. The Rolls Royce had been swapped for the friend's rather less conspicuous Standard Vanguard, and she and Jimmy were planning a tour of Scotland while establishing the residential qualifications needed before Scottish law would allow them to marry.

From the Carlton in Cannes, where he and his wife were staying, 'Monsieur le Major' later told reporters, 'The boys in my family are not in the habit of asking permission when they want to get married. My son Teddy, who is twenty-four, informed me that he was getting married only a few minutes before his wedding.' And no matter how great his private doubts that his son and future daughter-in-law were too young, the Major stuck to his policy of defending them throughout the next few weeks. After all, the Goldsmith honour too was now at stake. Why should anyone not think them suitable husbands?

Dismayed, but not put off, Senor Patino arrived in Edinburgh and established himself on the entire second floor of the Caledonian Hotel at the west end of Princes' Street, there to begin discussions with his lawyers and the private detectives he had hired to find his daughter. He was joined there by his wife, the Duchess of Durcal, which came as something of a surprise since Dom Antenor and his wife had enjoyed a distinctly strained relationship for very nearly the past decade. The Duchess had been suing him for divorce, and their arguments had become part of his daughter's life. Beseiged by his wife on one hand, and by the world's press on the other, Dom Antenor took to arriving at and leaving his hotel suite by the luggage lift.

On 29 December 1953, Jimmy and Isabel went to the Chief Registrar's Office in Edinburgh and posted formal notice of their intention to marry, then disappeared again. They were not legally obliged to state which Registrar in the south of Scotland they would be going to for the cere-mony. Antenor Patino responded at once. As soon as the New Year celebrations were over, he sought an interim interdict from the High Court preventing the issue of a marriage certificate to the couple. His application was granted, and immediately Jimmy Goldsmith gave notice of appeal – although he did not come out of hiding to do so.

Had Antenor Patino but known it, his daughter was less than four miles away. Undetected by the 130 pressmen, or by the private detectives, Jimmy Goldsmith and Isabel Patino were staying quietly at the Prestonfield House Hotel in the south-western suburbs of Edinburgh. It was there they had celebrated Hogmanay and settled down to wait the further week required of them by Scottish law before they could get married. In a house once used by Bonnie Prince Charlie to hide from his pursuers, they spent their time playing cards and reading. Isabel was still wearing the

46

neat black suit in which she had left Paris more than a fortnight before; there had been no opportunity to buy her a trousseau.

The newspapers were still full of their story. Jimmy Goldsmith and Isabel Patino had become instant celebrities, unwitting spokesmen for the new youth that was flowering in the wake of the austerity of war. Free, independent and intent on following their own instincts, no matter what the opposition, they symbolized a new generation, one which was proud of its romantic ideals and its passion.

To those who paid little or no attention to the story beyond the headlines it may have seemed that Jimmy Goldsmith was no more than a plausible young playboy who was intent on grabbing with both hands his chance of an easy life by marrying a beautiful and rich young woman. It was a misunderstanding that was to wound him deeply. For in reality his love for Isabel Patino was overwhelming. The suggestion that he was no more than an adventurer, which had been heightened by what seemed Antenor Patino's snobbish disregard for his family's history, was to make him feel afterwards that he could never be fully understood; and it bred in him for the first time a suspicion of anyone who sought to pry into his affairs.

But those thoughts were a long way from his mind when finally on 7 January 1954, Isabel Patino spoke to her mother on the telephone. By then it had become clear that an impasse had been reached: the appeal against Dom Antenor's injunction had been accepted, the couple were free to marry. Defeated by the mountainous publicity, and by his future son-in-law's determination not to be put off by threats or legal action, Dom Antenor had accepted that a compromise was inevitable. The tearful reconciliation between Isabel and her mother that morning was followed by wishes of good luck.

Shortly before four o'clock, as the grey Edinburgh dusk drew in, Jimmy Goldsmith and Isabel Patino slipped out of the Prestonfield House Hotel, drove down its gravel drive, and turned south. To escape any passing newspapermen, they were riding in the back of a butcher's van. Just over an hour later the van delivered them to the Registrar's

Office in the granite and cobbled town of Kelso, some forty miles south of the city in Sir Walter Scott's beloved border country. At 5.30 that afternoon, with the bride still wearing the simple black two-piece suit and the bridegroom sporting his fur-collared coat, their fantasy was fulfilled. They were married, but not a flashbulb greeted them at the door. They had escaped the attentions of the world's press to the last.

Indeed it was not until the following day that they came out of hiding. With a style that was to typify him later in his life, Jimmy Goldsmith gave a lunch party at the George Hotel in the centre of Edinburgh, and invited a hundred people. On the way to his wedding reception he bought Isabel several pairs of nylon stockings, it was their first opportunity for three weeks to do anything as commonplace as go into a shop.

As Isabel Goldsmith sat down to a lunch of oysters, chicken in Cognac and crême glacée, she showed every sign of being utterly happy, while for his part her new husband looked triumphant, perhaps slightly mischievous, but just as much in love.

In the *Daily Mirror* Cassandra commented, 'Not since the Stone of Scone was swiped from underneath the Coronation Chair in Westminster Abbey had the public been treated to such a feast of sentimental fun.'

No one knew then just how short-lived that fun would turn out to be.

4. Young Isabel

Back in Paris Mr and Mrs James Goldsmith no longer seemed the recklessly romantic young couple they had appeared in the pages of the press. Instead they seemed just an ordinary young couple in love who held hands, laughed at their private jokes, and argued cheerfully about anything and everything; oblivious to almost everything around them, everything that is except the birth of their first child.

They were by no means wealthy, however. Whatever the cynics may have suspected about the playboy's intentions towards the heiress, he continued to declare to anyone who would listen, 'I do not want any part – not a half-penny – of the Patino fortune. I wouldn't touch it.' The remark was met with knowing smiles from those who did not know Jimmy Goldsmith's intense pride. It had become a matter of honour for him to prove to Senor Patino how wrong he had been to suspect that he, a Goldsmith whose history stretched back 400 years, was nothing but a fortune-hunter. This dedication to proving himself worthwhile haunted him for many years.

So with only a small pharmaceutical business, and bills for his elopement amounting to more than £2000, they experienced their small financial difficulties, especially as Antenor Patino had made it abundantly clear that he had no intention of providing his newly married daughter with any kind of support, financial or otherwise. She was to be disinherited.

Once again Major Frank Goldsmith came to the rescue. Just as he had given his son Teddy room in his own office in the Rue de la Paix to start the pharmaceutical company and allowed Jimmy to take it over, so now he provided his younger son with a suite in the Hotel Scribe large enough for his new wife to be comfortable in during her confinement. They were to use it for as long as they needed, and certainly while they looked for a home large enough for them and their baby. Isabel derived great comfort from the fact that although relations with her own father and mother were frosty, her new family showed every sign of taking her to their heart. The Major and his wife believed Isabel was a beautiful, charming girl, who made their son a delightful wife. They were right. Jimmy and Isabel may have argued about everything, as they had always done, but always without malice. Their friends nodded wisely at the clashes, whispering to each other that without the arguments neither would have been quite certain that they were alive.

Isabel's was not a particularly difficult pregnancy. Indeed her cheeks seemed to glow ever more joyfully with the passing weeks. There were occasional headaches, but she did not worry about them, and neither did her husband. Instead she planned for the birth, saw her friends in Paris, and looked for an apartment. In April she and Jimmy let it be known they were expecting a baby, and that they intended to leave shortly to spend the summer in Cannes before it arrived.

On the morning of Wednesday, 12 May 1954, however, those plans and hopes disappeared as Isabel was taken into the Hartmann Clinic suffering the effects of a massive stroke caused by a clot of blood on her brain. Less than four days later the fiery-eyed Bolivian girl with a spirit as quicksilver as her husband's was dead; and all Paris seemed to go into mourning. For just as Jimmy Goldsmith and Isabel Patino's marriage had captured the imagination of a generation and struck a chord in the minds of young people, so Isabel's death seemed the unfairest cut of all, a bitter end to the fairy tale that so many had lived through with them. No hopes for the future seemed quite as certain after her death. In particular, nothing seemed certain for her husband.

But as his wife's coffin was brought to the funeral from her father's home on the Rue d'Andigne, hardly a kilometre from his own birthplace, Jimmy Goldsmith faced the world with barely an emotion showing on his twenty-one-year-old face. He seemed hardly to notice the 600 people crowded into the L'Eglise St Honoré d'Eylau, or the throng outside. Although *Le Figaro* noted the next day that 'some 3000 people, the majority of them women and young girls pressed on to the pavements of the Place Victor Hugo outside making it necessary to call the police'.

The mourners took more than an hour to file past the catafalque bearing Isabel's embalmed body while the church echoed to Beethoven's funeral march. The congregation included five duchesses, a princess, two marquesses, two counts and the ambassadors of most of the South American states, as well as many members of the Rothschild family. But although most of them came up to him as they left the church, Goldsmith stood still and alone. As he was to say later, 'It was a greater shock than anyone can ever imagine.'

Less than two kilometres away at the Hartmann Clinic his baby daughter, whom he had decided to christen Isabel in memory of her mother, still lay in an incubator. She was to remain in it for the next seven weeks, a weak, nervous child, frightened by light or noise. But she was all that Jimmy Goldsmith had left of his wife, or Antenor Patino and his wife had in memory of their daughter.

After the funeral Major Goldsmith and his wife advised their son to get away from Paris. There was nothing he could do for his child, and he needed a rest, they told him; a break from the familiar surroundings that he and Gypsy had relished so much only a week before. It was advice he eventually accepted. In June he left Paris, first for Cannes, and later for Ghana in West Africa as a guest of the British MP Geoffrey Bing. But he did not leave until he had discussed the care of his child, first with his own mother and then with the Duchess of Durcal. After some thought, he agreed that the Duchess should have the child in her care for a few weeks as soon as she was well enough to come out of the hospital. And so it transpired. When he finally came back from Liberia in July, having started a small branch of his pharmaceutical company there, he started to visit his daughter and her maternal grandmother. They were staying in the Trianon Hotel in Versailles, in a suite quite large enough for Isabel and her new English nurse, Miss Deborah Cockbill, whom he had decided was an essential feature of his new family.

The visits were a success. The Duchess seemed genuinely pleased to see her son-in-law, and she was clearly delighted to have her grandchild in her care. So pleased, in fact, that as the month wore on she asked if she might keep her with her at the Trianon for a few more weeks. He agreed with barely a moment's hesitation.

Throughout August, in between looking for a flat and pressing ahead with his pharmaceutical company, he continued to visit his daughter in Versailles, usually on a Sunday afternoon, sometimes alone but more often than not taking his mother with him. By September he had found a flat on the fifth floor of 23 Rue Marbeau, overlooking the Bois de Boulogne. Large and comfortable, with three bedrooms and its own terrace, it was hardly the apartment the average twenty-one-year-old making his way in business might have leased, but Jimmy Goldsmith never acted like an average young man. He was not about to start now.

So by the middle of September 1954 he was ready to settle into his new home with his daughter. He told the Duchess of Durcal that if it were acceptable to her he would like to collect the child, together with Nurse Cockbill, on 15 September. It would be four months to the day after her birth. Without any hesitation the Duchess agreed.

But when he arrived at Versailles that Wednesday morning to collect his daughter, he found the door to the Trianon suite locked. He knocked but there was no reply. He knocked again. There was no sound from inside. By now in a rage, he knocked the door down and burst into the suite. There was no sign of his daughter, his mother-in-law, or his nurse. There was every sign they had left in a hurry.

Still in a rage he rushed back to his parents' suite at the Scribe to see his mother; and as he talked to her he paced the floor, shouting wildly, his blue eyes darkened with anger. He was determined that someone should be punished. As he had done nine months earlier when his anger had been roused by Antenor Patino, and as he was to do many more times in his life, he controlled the deep anger he felt by consulting his lawyers. Then, as now, the emotions he felt were expressed in the tone of his voice, the choice of his language; the violence was in his lawyers' actions.

That afternoon, four months to the day after his wife's death, he issued a writ in the civil court in Paris claiming that 'unknown persons' had kidnapped his child. It was the start of another drama which would be lived out in the public eye, another occasion on which he would feel a victim of circumstances, and feel as though he were fighting the establishment of France. He chose the only weapons he felt were truly at his disposal, the courts.

By the following morning, when *Le Figaro* first reported the details of a case which was to provoke almost as much excitement in Paris as the kidnapping of Charles Lindbergh's child had done thirty years earlier, it was quite clear that little Isabel Goldsmith was not really missing. As Jimmy Goldsmith had suspected, the Duchess of Durcal had issued separate custody proceedings at the same civil court. She claimed that her son-in-law was not a fit person to look after his child. The accusation deepened still further the resentment he already felt, and sharpened his determination not to be defeated.

In view of the seriousness of the matters, and the publicity it attracted, a hearing of the case was set for the following afternoon at the Palais de Justice on the Ile de la Cité, before the eminent Judge Ausset, President of the Tribunal Civil de la Seine. The Duchess of Durcal, however, was to be represented by the most renowned advocate in France, Maître René Floriot.

Sharp at three o' clock on Friday, 17 September, Judge Ausset took his seat in the panelled courtroom behind the gilt gates of the Palais de Justice and one of the most celebrated and widely reported custody actions ever to take place in France began, and one in which the Goldsmith name was to be severely questioned. For the Duchess of Durcal was claiming not only that her son-in-law 'travelled a lot' but also that this meant he could not give a child of four months the vigilant care she required.

Outside the court Maître Floriot told *Le Figaro*, 'I will certainly not miss making the point that since the beginning of July Madame Patino has had care of the baby with the total accord of the father. One is thus surprised that he now suddenly wants to take back little Isabel.' For his part Goldsmith was telling his friends, 'The Patinos want the whole thing hushed up, but I'll be damned if I'll hush it up.'

Inevitably the clash between Floriot and the young Goldsmith was to be the focal point of the hearing. Floriot told the court, 'Monsieur Goldsmith is convinced that we want to take away his child and indeed that we have already taken her to Spain. What a mistake! But it is only that when Madame Patino saw her son-in-law in a state of excitement of which he later provided abundant proof by forcing the door at the Hotel Trianon she decided to put the little girl in security, fearing that her father would take her away at the risk of her already fragile life.'

In reply Goldsmith explained, 'My child was taken to an unknown place. They have literally kidnapped her, which makes me very angry.' His own advocate, the more restrained Maître Alle-Haut, then added on his behalf that 'he alone had the right to determine who should care for his child'. 'And the excited state he is in, for which he is being reproached, in fact demonstrates his affection for his daughter.'

Looking faintly bewildered by the charge and counter charge, Judge Ausset asked Maître Floriot if he might know the whereabouts of the child. 'I will tell you, but not in front of Monsieur Goldsmith,' Floriot replied. Jimmy Goldsmith was beside himself. In retaliation he suggested from the witness box that his own mother had lived a blameless 'bourgeois existence' for thirty years, whereas the Duchess of Durcal was suing her husband for divorce.

Nevertheless he remained calm enough to explain to Judge Ausset that he had rented a five-roomed apartment on the Rue Marbeau, so that his daughter would have her own large and sunny room, and there would also be accommodation for her nanny. He also told the court that his mother was prepared to come and live with him and her grandchild Isabel at the apartment to ensure that the little girl received every proper attention.

Outside the court he was distinctly less restrained. He

was now threatening to sue the Patino family for defamation of character, and was telling his friends, 'They said it was not good enough for my baby – three bathrooms, a veranda, a cook and a valet.'

Still clearly bewildered, Judge Ausset decided that he had best see for himself the apartment that Mr Goldsmith had described as a suitable home for his daughter. He informed both sides to the action that the following morning he would visit the Rue Marbeau, and that after the visit he would deliver his verdict.

So shortly after ten o' clock the following morning, a Saturday, a considerable crowd gathered outside the Palais de Justice, blocking traffic. The previous afternoon's extraordinary hearing had been extremely widely reported, although to Jimmy Goldsmith's annoyance some of the Paris newspapers had repeated the well-worn description of him as a playboy. But, ever inquisitive, the Parisians had turned up in force to see for themselves the characters in the courtroom drama. When half an hour later Judge Ausset, the court officials and the parties to the action set off across Paris to visit the narrow street in the 16 ième arrondissement to inspect the top floor of Number 23, they were followed by a fascinated crowd. When they arrived they discovered that as well as the accommodation its owner had described, it also boasted a magnificent view across the Boulevard de Admiral Bruix to the Bois de Boulogne, whose trees had not yet turned to the rust of autumn.

His inspection over, Judge Ausset announced quickly that he would deliver his judgement at two o'clock that afternoon at the Palais de Justice. Outside the crowd grew steadily until by lunchtime the road had become impassable. Promptly at two, however, Judge Ausset entered the civil court. Jimmy Goldsmith and his mother sat impassively on one side of the courtroom. The Duchess of Durcal and Antenor Patino sat opposite them. Neither side looked at the other as the Judge began to speak softly.

He told the court that the apartment he had seen that morning on the Rue Marbeau was comfortable, 'even luxurious', that it had the benefit of being airy, and had a terrace. He went on to say that Mrs Goldsmith had promised to occupy herself 'maternally' with the child in question, and that she had presented 'substantial moral qualities' to the court.

Antenor Patino and his wife were visibly unsettled by Judge Ausset's remarks, as they implied support for their son-in-law's case. Their discomfort grew as the judgement wore on. For the judge went on to explain that the young man, whose daughter was the subject of the custody proceedings, was clearly in an 'enviable financial situation', and that the excitement he had shown at the Hotel Trianon was clearly as a result of his distress and his anxiety to know the whereabouts of his daughter. Finally, after twenty minutes, Judge Ausset announced his decision that the child should be returned to her father before four o'clock the following afternoon.

Jimmy Goldsmith's jubilation was clear for the entire courtroom to see. Floriot had been vanquished, and so had the Patino family – for the second time; the law was indeed a defence against the force of accepted wisdom from the establishment. It was a lesson the young plaintiff would not forget.

This time, however, there were to be no reconciliations between the two sides. The Patino family left in silence, not speaking to the Goldsmiths, after Floriot had indicated to the court that they intended to appeal against the decision. Judge Ausset accepted the statement but repeated his instructions that the tiny Isabel Goldsmith should be returned to her father by four the following afternoon. Among the crowd outside, arguments raged over who should have won, the playboy or the grandmother. Both sides were right was the common verdict. Neither should have lost.

5. The Slimming Business

Yet again Jimmy Goldsmith had found his life the focus of public curiosity, a source of public speculation. For the second time in a year he found himself presented in the newspapers, and in a court of law, as a petulant, irresponsible, and argumentative young man who was probably a great deal too rich, and far too idle for someone of just twenty-one years of age. No matter how just the cause he was pursuing, he was painted a reckless playboy with little better to occupy him than the pursuit of gambling and beautiful, rich young women.

It was an image that he would never escape throughout the rest of his career, perhaps because it did represent something of the truth about a section of his character. His appetite for a glamorous, extravagant life did attract publicity; and his instinct for the extravagant gesture hardly diminished the attraction. The fact that he had been brought up to know no other life than one of wealth and leisure made the harsh description of him all the more difficult to bear. The idea that he should have understood that his world was different from the average did not occur to him.

But equally the description of him as an arrogant young playboy ignored the shyness in his character that all the bluster and arm waving of his public appearances was designed to conceal; a frailty which the court cases had concealed, but which was there nonetheless. Why else would he try so hard to be noticed if he did not in part wish to hide? Later in his life he would acknowledge the ambivalence and reverse the process, becoming almost obsessively secretive while wishing to be noticed.

The ordeal of the Paris custody action for his daughter Isabel demonstrated to him that publicity brought its pain as well as its reputation; in particular in its invasion of his privacy. What started out as an adventure as he eloped with Isabel Patino had become a burden. So the boy who had liked the limelight chose instead to become a man who preferred the shadows – for the next few years at least.

His restless spirit remained, however, as did his volcanic temper, as well as the desire he had demonstrated since boyhood to dominate everyone he met with the force of his own personality. Yet after the custody action he brought even these dramatic, adolescent qualities under control. They were never to leave him altogether, but he learned instead to restrain them in order to prove that he deserved to be taken a great deal more seriously than a playboy with too little or nothing to occupy his time.

In the next years he harnessed the aggression he felt at the insults unfairly thrown against him by directing his energy into business. He vowed that he would prove that the Patino family had been wrong. His critics would learn that the charming young man who lost his temper was in reality much more serious than he appeared.

Indeed it was to become a legend in the Goldsmith family that he would not go out for the next five years so determined was he to make a success of his business career; and that every evening, instead of returning to his old habits, he would settle into his father's office in the Rue de la Paix and devote himself to getting the tiny company he had taken over from his brother Teddy, now renamed by him Laboratoires Cassene, off the ground.

Certainly the pattern of his life had changed with his new flat, and the return of his tiny daughter and her English nurse. There were not the endless excursions to the popular Elephant Blanc Club as there had been in the past and there was a vigorous investigation of how to expand not only the rheumatism cream but also the launching of other products, but life was not entirely work with no play. There were trips to the Crillon Bar not far from the office at lunchtime and the odd chat with the journalist Sam White. Talk of whom he might have seen, or what he might have heard. There were also invitations to dinner and the weekend, though he treated them cautiously, because, probably for the first time in his life, he had come to understand that some people did not entirely approve of his actions or his style, no matter how hard he may have tried to persuade them they were wrong. He decided to remain within the safety of his own group of friends, who remained loyal to him. It was a decision he would not change.

Undeniably his business absorbed his energies. Unexpectedly perhaps, he discovered that it could provide him with almost as much enjoyment as gambling, and indeed he could even treat it in a similar way. But most of all he realized he wanted to make his mark, and to make it quickly.

In the two years that his brother was away in the army Jimmy Goldsmith expanded the tiny firm from having just one employee to employing a hundred; from one product into a range. He borrowed money where and when he could, grabbing whatever assets he could lay his hands on, and making the best possible use of them. Not content with remaining a distribution company for pharmaceutical products, he expanded into manufacturing products under licence, and in the two and a half years after his wife's death he did so as rapidly as his limited resources would allow, taking into his company on the way products that were to become household names in Europe, including Lantigen B and Alka Seltzer. It was all done with the energy of a man in a desperate, all-consuming hurry, for whom nothing could ever wait. Every opportunity or idea had to be exploited immediately, in case someone else took advantage of it. As he was to put it later, he had 'loads of energy but no experience. I expanded too fast with no capital and no knowledge of finance and had to pay the consequences.'

The breakneck pace of the expansion meant that it did not take long for him to come up against the rather more traditional drug companies. At first they may have viewed his activities with little more than mild interest, but very soon that attitude changed to one of suspicion which in turn became a sharp sense of disquiet. 'I had not sufficiently taken into account the reactions of the big pharmaceutical companies,' he remembers now. 'They did not take too kindly to me.' In particular he realized suddenly that he depended on the banks to sustain his rapid expansion, and although they had been only too happy to help a small business getting on its feet, they were rather less certain about supporting someone determined to overturn a commercial structure which had been operating successfully for years.

After two years of trying to break the drug companies' hold on the market, in the words of one of his friends, 'the banks began to turn off the tap on him'. The decision later rankled with Goldsmith and reinforced a suspicion that he was forever destined to be regarded as an outsider, someone never to be afforded the entire privileges of the establishment, no matter how hard he might work to deserve them. By the summer of 1957, as the need for further capital became more acute, the speed of the expansion in Laboratoires Cassene had begun to slow. There were no resources to fall back on. In July it had become clear that he had overstretched himself, and that the bills of exchange due to be presented at the banks of Paris in the next weeks could not be met. Jimmy Goldsmith was on the verge of going bankrupt.

On 13 July 1957 he was convinced that the following day the possibility would become a reality, and that all his ambitions would have turned to dust. In a daze, he went home to his new apartment in the Rue de Lubeck. 'I fully expected to be declared a bankrupt next day, when the bills were presented at the banks,' he recalls. 'And that was a great deal more serious in France then than it has become.' He believed there was every chance that he would never again be able to operate in business.

That night he decided to forget his troubles; not by gambling, but by going to see a film with echoes of his own father's Edwardian life, Mike Todd's *Around the World in Eighty Days* starring David Niven which had just opened in Paris on the Champs Elysée. After it finished he had a drink in the Traveller's Club at Number 25 and went home to bed, to await his fate. 'In the circumstances I slept fairly well, but I didn't bother to get up very early. There didn't seem much point. I just had breakfast slowly, and finally, after a while, I went out to buy a paper. I fully expected to see it saying, "Goldsmith Bankrupt" in the headlines,' he says now.

Instead, the headlines simply read, 'Bank Strike'. 'I

couldn't believe it. While the strike was on during the next eighteen days or so I managed to sell most of my interests in the business to one of my major competitors, Laboratoires Roussell,' he remembers. 'Since then I've always viewed strikes with peculiarly mixed feelings.'

The sale of most of Cassenne raised nearly £100,000, and ensured that he met every debt when the banks opened again; but more important than the narrowest of escapes, the events gave him a considerable fright, convincing him that, however it might appear, business was to be treated with financial caution, regardless of his gambler's instincts. 'We had been an enormous commercial success, but a financial failure,' he says now. After that Bastille Day he became determined never to be caught in the same way again.

Nevertheless Laboratoires Cassene convinced him that the pharmaceutical industry still had possibilities, some of which might well lie in England, where he had already been experimenting with a small drug company called Ward Casson, whose chairman was the Labour MP Julian Ward. In the next eighteen months he put more and more effort into his English operation. One drug which he dealt with was a new version of the drug cortisone, which had itself only been introduced a short time earlier for the treatment of rheumatoid arthritis.

'Ward Casson,' he said later, 'marketed a number of cortisone derivatives which were fairly new and which were known as deltacortisone or prednisone. These had recently been discovered by an American company called Schering, which had obtained worldwide patents for their discovery and had licensed a number of major companies throughout the world to produce the raw material, prednisone, according to their specifications and under their patent.'

The major licence holders then reached an agreement with each other whereby one would produce the raw material in each country and then sell it to the others, who would use it in their products. His English company, Ward Casson, bought its raw materials from Laboratoires Roussel, which had a major manufacturing plant in England. It proceeded to cut the price for a thousand deltacortisone tablets from £60 to £12. Once again he ran straight into the formidable opposition of the established drug companies.

In December 1958 his delta-cortisone tablets were subjected to a barrage of criticism in the *Lancet*, and shortly afterwards these criticisms were taken up in the House of Commons.

A doctor in the *Lancet* criticized them as being cheap imported products, which was not true. As Jimmy Goldsmith said later, 'The tablets were manufactured in Britain on behalf of Ward Casson. They were not imported. They were the same raw material as everybody else had and they were manufactured in Britain. The only crime was that we broke the cartel among the major drug companies and sold the products to British hospitals at a price which gave up a good profit but which was well below the cartel prices. The only unusual thing about them was that they were less expensive.'

Nevertheless, the criticisms had their impact on his business, now part of a small public company called Clinical and General Industries. As 1959 progressed, it became increasingly clear that the prospects of Clinical and General were not growing any rosier, even though he had refuted the claims that his tablets were sub-standard. Not for the first or the last time, the public image of being a young man in too much of a hurry to be entirely trustworthy caught up with his business.

By now aged twenty-six, he was left with the conviction that there was a conspiracy among the establishment against him; and that no matter how much energy or entrepreneurial skill he might demonstrate he seemed destined to encounter obstacles almost too great to be overcome, placed in his path by those who did not trust him. But he was not about to give up. There was nothing he relished more than a fight.

Besides, in France, at least, he did not seem to be so alone. He had acquired a new supporter and friend, who had arrived in the dark days of 1957. In the middle of the year a bank had quietly opened its doors on the ground floor of Number 23, Rue de la Paix, the building occupied by his father's office, which he still shared. The 'Banque d'Arbitrage et de Credit' was under the direction of Selim Zilkha, a thirty-year-old Iraq-born financier, who was working in the City of London, but who had connections in France. Anxious for customers, the new bank had sent leaflets advertising its services to every tenant in the block. Naturally, one of the recipients of the leaflet was Jimmy Goldsmith.

Rather than appear desperate, he waited a week before investigating the possibility. He did not go downstairs and ask what they might be able to offer him if he were to become their client. Instead he invited them upstairs and asked, 'What can I do to help you?' Brass cheek or not, the bank on the ground floor was most grateful. His plans to expand and his need for finance to support such developments made him exactly the sort of person in whom the bank, keen to establish a foothold among the new breed of French businessmen, was interested. So much so that when Selim Zilkha enquired from London whom his new bank had managed to recruit, he was told about Mr James Goldsmith; who had in turn asked about the bank's directors. In the next two years the two men were to become not only business partners but friends.

So when the criticism of his cortisone tablets persisted in England in 1959 and it became clear that a move into a new field might be inevitable, he asked his newly acquired banker if he might like to be involved in a new project. He already had a scheme worked out, he told Zilkha, and was just completing the negotiations for it. Even though he had no clear idea of how he was going to finance it, he knew it would work. He had agreed to buy twenty-eight old-fashioned chemist's shops in England which Sir Charles Clore owned as part of the Mappin and Webb group of companies he had just taken over. The shops, called Lewis and Burrows, needed modernization but he felt they would be the ideal foundation for a new type of chemist's chain. As a drug manufacturer and importer, he believed he had some knowledge of how it might be achieved. So in December 1959 Zilkha agreed to stop being a banker and become his partner. For the next two years they were to sit opposite each other at a desk every day, creating what was to become the Mothercare chain of shops.

Life was not all business, however. Jimmy Goldsmith was still a gambler by instinct and inclination, though more at cards and backgammon than horses now. He liked to gamble with his friend from Walton Street, Oxford, John Aspinall, who was still running private parties, but was also considering starting his own gaming club when the British gaming laws were changed, as they seemed destined to be in the near future.

There were also one or two young and usually beautiful women, but no serious attachments. For while the memory of Isabel's death had still lingered in his mind, he had spent most of his time working alongside his secretary, Ginette Lery, the daughter of a Paris Metro worker. Over the first years of the pharmaceutical company, and its attendant traumas, Ginette had remained one of the few stable features in his life, eternally solid and reliable, working for his success, even though she had heard him describe himself as 'the capitalist without capital' from time to time. As his business had grown, so had their relationship deepened. Struggling alone against the financial world meant that he spent long hours with the comparatively small, slight girl with soft voice and gentle eyes, who had never really encountered anyone like the tall young man in a hurry in her life before. By 1958 they were living together and in May 1959 Ginette bore them a son, whom they christened Manes. Although they were not married, the Goldsmith family could now look upon its most rebellious young member as having at least the beginnings of a proper and respectable family life.

Perhaps the birth of his son put the notion of clothes for the mother-to-be and her child into his mind, no one is quite sure, but within a year he and Selim Zilkha had opened the first department with that as their objective in one of their newly acquired chemist's shops. From these Mothercare developed. In March 1961 the two partners bought a further chain of fifty pram and nursery furniture shops which were just about to close down. Meanwhile they had also decided to open two new shops at Ealing and Kingston in London's more affluent suburbs to test their idea for departments for mothers and children. It turned out to be an expensive process. There were losses to be met, and as the idea grew, so did the losses. In the first two years they lost some £200,000 and its two owners had to find ways of financing their idea.

Selim Zilkha, with his background in banking, was in rather a better position to support the expansion than his partner, who was not only six years younger but rather less well-off. By the end of 1961 it was clear that Jimmy Goldsmith could not keep up with his partner in supplying their venture with financial support. The more he failed to do so, the less he remained an equal partner, and Goldsmith was determined not to be anything less than an equal partner. As 1961 drew to a close and the Ealing shop opened, he was aware that before long he would be forced into accepting a minority shareholding because of his own lack of resources. He would never accept that. So in the first week of 1962 Jimmy Goldsmith decided to sell his shares to his partner. In return he would buy out Zilkha's share in a business they had started together in France called Lanord.

He had decided to return to what he felt he knew better, France, and the manufacturing industry. He would try to exploit an idea he had seen in America, a slimming product called Metrecal. Already within the Lanord company he had taken over a small laboratory with the name Milical, and he decided this should form the base of the new product in France; but once again a drug company took exception to his ideas.

This time the American producers of Metrecal issued a suit against him for using their ideas. Undeterred, and as anxious as ever to defend himself, especially in court, he launched a cheeky suit against the American company for using his company's name. The Milical name and company, he argued, had been in existence for many years, certainly far longer than the American product. He was not using their idea, they had used his name. He won the case. As a result, Milical was to become the single most important product in his French company over the next years, the first foundation of his commercial success.

Milical was not his only product, however. Within Lanord he had also decided to exploit another American idea, the new craze for a cream which guaranteed a suntan without spending hours in the sun. Known in the United States as Man Tan, he brought it to France as Right Tan. It was typical of his business style at the time to take a brand name, preferably one with a reputation, and try to exploit it. This was a technique to which he would return.

Even though he was no longer in business there, England was where he chose to relax. Jimmy Goldsmith was still keen on 'making whoopee', as he called it, when the opportunity presented itself, and though he preferred the company of his male friends, such as Selim Zikha and John Aspinall, much as his father had before him, there were still the delights of beautiful women.

So as the Conservative Government of Harold Macmillan stood by its election claim and tried to ensure that people 'never had it so good', Jimmy Goldsmith spent as much time as he could in Britain enjoying himself, and looking at the prospects of returning there in business.

The new Clermont Club in Berkeley Square, which had been opened by John Aspinall, was getting into its stride, and downstairs another of his Eton contemporaries, but not a close friend, Mark Birley, was about to open a nightclub and restaurant, and name it after his wife, Annabel, a daughter of the Marquis of Londonderry. Both were to play an important part in Jimmy Goldsmith's life.

The Clermont, housed in the last William Kent house in London, designed in 1742, became one of the regular venues of his relaxation; where he could play backgammon and cards in a magnificently ornate setting, aware that his privacy would always be respected, that he was among friends who would seldom criticize his actions, and upon whose loyalty and discretion he could rely. It was a closed world and they were a set of friends to whom he himself remained loyal throughout the next twenty years. From the brooding days of the 1950s when Isabel's death was still fresh in his mind had emerged a confident businessman with a taste for parties, who would become the most successful member of the circle of friends who met at the Clermont.

It was one of his parties that briefly returned him to the public eye at this period. In May 1961 John Aspinall had decided to celebrate Derby Day as he usually did – by giving a particularly spectacular party for 150 of his friends; and he asked Jimmy Goldsmith if he could hold it in a marquee outside his rented house just off Regent's Park. Goldsmith duly warned the residents of his street and hired Maples the furnishers to erect the tent. What he neglected to tell his neighbours was that the tent was in the shape of an Indian temple, and was so large it would take a team of men more than a week to erect.

'It's so huge it looks like a village,' one of the road's anguished residents remarked as the dome of the marquee rose seventy feet from the ground. The canvas structure alone cost him £12,500. As his neighbours collected signatures in protest, he remained impassive and smiling whenever they remonstrated with him, ignoring the questions of reporters sent to cover the story. He studiously did not tell them it was John Aspinall's party, not his: the fun of the publicity was too great for that.

It was also in London that he met one of the women who was briefly to consume his life, the singularly beautiful model Sally Crichton Stuart. For slightly more than two years they lived together in London, while Ginette continued to bring up Manes in France. Marriage may have been discussed but it never took place. Instead, in 1963 he quietly married Ginette Lery, and in January 1964 she gave birth to a daughter, whom they called Alix, in honour of his new business partner, his cousin Baron Alexis de Gunzburg.

Some of his friends in England believed that Jimmy Goldsmith never intended to remain married in France, and that his heart was in England with Sally. But as 1963 turned into 1964 and his daughter Alix was born, it became quite clear to them that he saw no contradiction in sustaining one affair in England and a marriage in France. Early in 1964 his relationship with Sally began to dissolve, but even after her marriage to the Aga Khan, they remained friends. For a time Ginette and her two children came to stay with him in England, but before long she gratefully returned to France, to a house they had found on the Left

Bank, near that massive monument to Louis XIV and later to Napoleon, Les Invalides. Firmly respectable, with its handsome courtyard and magnificent ceilings, it had once belonged to the songwriter Cole Porter; and it became his permanent Paris home.

Unassuming, shy, yet fiercely loyal and more determined to hang on to her new husband than many who met her gave her credit for, Ginette Lery remained not only his defender and supporter, but also his wife, far longer than any of his friends believed possible in 1964. To those who saw the marriage only from the outside it might have seemed unbalanced, a shy woman from a quiet home and a voluble young man born and bred in the hotel suites of Europe. But to him it represented a sense of solidity, and of family, which he valued much more highly than many suspected. In this, he was typical of the Goldschmidts of Frankfurt, a tribe who had always accepted their responsibilities to all who came within their territory, be they women, children or friends.

By the end of 1963 his commercial fortunes had begun to settle down. The Lanord company which controlled Milical and Right Tan had become Gustin Milical, with a profit of more than £100,000 a year, and for the first time it seemed certain that he would survive. But Goldsmith was still haunted by the memory of his Bastille Day in 1957 and, to everyone's surprise, he decided to sell a third of his business.

He explained later, 'I wanted to consolidate so that if things fell off again, I would not be in danger of going broke.' Just before his daughter Alix was born he sold a third of Gustin Milical, which was then well on the way to dominating the slimming-foods market in France, to his cousin from the Russian strain in the family, Baron Alexis de Gunzburg, whose grandmother was his great aunt and whose grandfather had created the French Shell Oil company. The price he received was paid largely in shares in Source Perrier, the French mineral water, and in a coffee company.

The deal enabled him to gird his loins for what he had been considering for some time, a move back into business in Britain. At the time when The Beatles had just reached

Number One with 'She Loves You', and the 'swinging six-ties' seemed to be on everyone's lips, he decided that England could prove the springboard from which he could create a financial empire – and an international reputation. Such success would bring with it something beyond prize: power and influence.

6. Cavenham's Master Builder

It was the Spring of 1964 when Lady Annabel Birley first really noticed Jimmy Goldsmith. He had been around for a while in her husband's club, Annabel's, but she had not paid much attention to him, in spite of the gossip about his affair with Sally Crichton Stuart. She was twenty-nine and had a great many other things on her mind.

For a start there were her three children, Rupert, Robin and Jane, all under ten: and then there was her husband Mark, whom she had married ten years before just after 'coming out' as a debutante. His life and hers no longer really coincided. She was busy during the day with the children; he worked at night in the club, and slept for at least part of every day. It was not quite the marriage she had envisaged during their two-month honeymoon in Kitzbühel early in 1954.

Tall, with strong features, Annabel Birley was a Londonderry, the youngest child of the 8th Marquis, brought up in the heart of the British aristocracy. Its certainty and calm were a natural part of her heritage. There was no need to fight to make a name, no need for the bluster of James Goldsmith. A place in the world had been hers by right of the simple fact of her birth.

Even if that had not been the case, Annabel Birley would still have made her mark. She was as fierce and independent as the Londonderrys had always been, capable not only of knowing her own mind, but also of making sure her thoughts were translated into action. Strikingly beautiful, the passion had shown in her eyes even as a girl at the great balls of the debutante season in 1952 when she and Elizabeth Leicester had been given a dinner by the new Queen Elizabeth as her first private engagement after King George VI's death. But Annabel Birley had not slipped into the mindless circuit of modelling and Caribbean holidays, of a string of elegible admirers each offering the blandishments of elegant weekends on the country estate, in between the gay whirl of London, as so many of her contemporaries had done. Instead she had fallen in love, married and accepted her new role as mother with pride and pleasure.

Although Goldsmith was also the proud, indeed doting, father of three children, there the similarities between them ended. Restless and unconventional, with a wild reputation, and the habits of a nomad, shifting from city to city and from hotel suite to hotel suite, he was expansive, eternally talkative, and with a desire to dominate that swept most people before it. Yet it did not sweep Annabel Birley off her feet. Instead she stood up to the slightly vain young man who seemed never to stop pacing up and down. In France his wife Ginette might have tried gently to persuade him; in England Annabel Birley clashed with him head on.

Opposites they may have appeared, but in the summer of 1964, after meeting in her husband's club, they fell in love. She felt convinced that beneath the brashness there was a vulnerability and a tenderness that his children also saw, even if others doubted.

For the next two years their affair was conducted with complete discretion, and yet it was every bit as important to him as the development of his business. Indeed ironically over the next fifteen years his business commitments in England and his relationship with Lady Annabel Birley were to run along parallel lines. Both began in a small quiet way, became large and extremely public, were legally consolidated, and then took a new course.

But when the couple met that night in the summer of 1964, Goldsmith was a long way from being an established businessman in England. His return from France to restart his commercial life was not the invasion of a massive financial army, with a strategy prepared by a general rich in resources of manpower or money. It was rather the arrival of a mercenary commando force with nothing to lose and a great deal to gain by mounting a coup to take the heights of the financial establishment of Britain. Risk was part of the attraction.

The base for the assault on the commanding heights of British industry was to be Gustan Milical with its successful range of slimming and pharmaceutical products, which were making their owner profits of about £120,000 a year in France. The tactics he intended to use were exactly those he had refined over the past decade in France – to find weak companies in difficulties, take them over, develop their potential with new management, sell off those assets which did not help their principal objective, and use the new company and the cash raised as the stepping stone for the next take-over. His ground rules were still absolutely clear: he would never accept less than a majority shareholding, and he would try never to let the momentum of acquisition stumble while conditions in the stock market were right. It was an attack that resembled the plan of a mercenary in a hurry to take the capital before the defenders had a chance to organize.

Indeed, it was timing that now became his prime interest. The rush to build an empire was inspired by a conviction that the beneficial financial climate would only continue for a limited period of time. Some stock market analysts might shake their heads in six years' time in disbelief at the speed of his invasion, but he would point out that there was no alternative. The time had come when it was possible. Sceptics could call that the pragmatic explanation of an opportunist determined to make a swift killing in Britain, but he dismissed the thought as a misunderstanding of the need to get any movement under way at the right time.

So with the reassurance of Alexis de Gunzburg's financial support from the sale of a third of his French company, and using money borrowed from Isaac Wolfson, Jimmy Goldsmith set out to seize the time in 1964, and conquer British industry. He chose to do it in the unlikely area of food, first manufacturing it, and later selling it. He would make excursions into other fields over the years, such as property, banking and insurance, but in England he would always return to food. For in his mind he had a notion that Europe could sustain another major food combine, a rival to the gigantic Unilever and Nestlé, and he believed he could create it.

So as 1964 began in England, with the unlikely person of Sir Alec Douglas Home as the new Conservative Prime

Minister, Jimmy Goldsmith began to buy companies. He started quietly by buying the slimming bread, Procea, in March, Carson's chocolates in June, the old-established biscuit-makers, Carr's of Carlisle, in October and, finally, just at the end of the year, a stake in J. A. & P. Holland (renowned for gumming up the teeth of generations of English schoolchildren with its product Walter's Palm Toffee). Then in January 1965 he bought Elizabeth Shaw chocolates and soon afterwards the Goodies and Yeatman companies. In July 1965 he took complete control of Carson's chocolates and Holland's toffees.

As the *Sunday Times* commented six years later, 'Within nineteen months, from small beginnings, Goldsmith had constructed a £27 million a year group.' It was a spectacular invasion, but one which attracted a good deal of scepticism. To the principal figures of the City of London it looked altogether the work of a young man in too much of a hurry. They suspected that he would do nothing but harm, would disappear within a few months after taking his profit, and that he would demonstrate financial ruthlessness rather than sound commercial judgement. Events were to prove the sceptics wrong, but that was not to affect their opinion.

In particular, his image as a playboy lingered on. He did nothing to dispel this image: he saw no reason to temper his actions or his lifestyle to appease an establishment which, he was convinced, would never approve of him. He decided instead to tread his own path and ignore any doubts which might be expressed about him. It was a decision which would eventually rebound on him, for it misunderstood the British need to take rebels into the establishment.

He decided to call his new group of companies when it came together in August 1965 after the rush of acquisition, Cavenham Foods, in memory of his grandfather's estate in Suffolk. As the chairman, he stated in the companies second annual report in December 1966: 'At the outset Cavenham owned fifty-one active companies, which, in the main, operated independently.' He went on to explain that his company's sole objective was to be 'manufacturing food and wholesaling confectionery and tobacco'. Any other activities in the firms he had taken over would be sold or closed. This was not the kind of business his more illustrious cousins the Rothschilds had ever been involved in but it represented a bridgehead in England, and he intended to capitalize on it as quickly as he could. Taking in the distribution part of the Holland toffee company, and with the help of one of the City of London's rather more respected bright young men, Jim Slater (who sold him his 20 per cent holding), Goldsmith launched a £1·4 million bid for the tobacco and confectionery wholesaler Singleton and Cole, which had an annual turnover of £22 million. His intention was to create a wholesaling division for his new Cavenham group of companies. The new, larger Cavenham, he predicted, would have an annual turnover of £37 million – £25 million from tobacco, £10 million from sweets and £2 million from other miscellaneous goods. The take-over went smoothly enough, but then his troubles began.

For once his timing was not particularly good. The sudden introduction of Selective Employment Tax by Harold Wilson's Labour Government (elected in 1964) cost Singleton and Cole £90,000 in a full year. Neither did the business prove easy to reorganize. He had adopted a management style he was to stick to – not taking any part in the detailed administration of his businesses – but his comparatively new management team was struggling to make sense of their chairman's latest acquisition. The new Cavenham now had 5000 employees in four divisions, making everything from sugar mice to the Royal Family's favourite water biscuits, but its conglomeration of companies lacked a joint sense of direction.

From the beginning, the confectionary division's many parts provided the new small board of the company, which included Jimmy Goldsmith as chairman and joint managing director and Baron Alexis de Gunzburg as deputy chairman, with a perpetual headache. Sugar mice were not their saviour. Nevertheless, the four directors optimistically entered into an agreement with the French public company Source Perrier (which, as well as controlling Perrier, was also the largest manufacturer of soft drinks in Europe) to unite their troublesome division with

Perrier's equally difficult confectionary division into a new partnership to exploit the European market. The agreement was made easier by the fact that Alexis de Gunzberg was also a director and a major shareholder in Perrier. But it failed to raise any money or solve the problem, and there was the even more pressing problem of Singleton and Cole to contend with.

So at the same time as forming a link with Perrier, Goldsmith formed another partnership, this time with the American Conwood Corporation of Memphis, Tennessee. Together with Conwood, he set up a Swiss company, called Conwood SA, with 50 per cent of its shares held by each of the two partners. The profitable snuff interests in Singleton and Cole were then passed into the Swiss company, and as a result Cavenham received a payment of £811,241. But in spite of even these typically elaborate financial manoeuvrings Cavenham was still in serious difficulties. The forecasts made by its directors were simply not going to be met, and an injection of capital was badly needed. Finally Roland Franklin, a director himself, and also a representative of the company's merchant bankers Keyser Ullman, came to the conclusion that the directors themselves had to inject half a million pounds into the company if it were to survive. After a little heartsearching he and Alexis de Gunzburg, the two principal directors, agreed to do so, and they decided to make an outright 'gift' to the company. It was a desperate measure, and hardly the style of a man later to be called a financial genius, but there was no alternative.

Jimmy Goldsmith did not find it easy to find a quarter of a million pounds. Successful French businessman he may have been, but he was not in the millionaire class of his cousin Alexis. It was not exactly the last penny he had in the world – there were still some shares in the family hotel company (although fewer than £200,000-worth for the whole Goldsmith family including his father, mother and brother Teddy, but not a great deal else. Gustin Milical was bringing him a profit of about £120,000 a year, but he had an expensive lifestyle to support, including three children and a wife in France, not to mention his affair in England. But Jimmy Goldsmith was not about to sacrifice his lifestyle for anyone. He had never done so in the past and he saw no reason to do so now.

The gift of £500,000 saved the company, but it did not entirely eradicate its difficulties. When the company's 1966 annual report was published in December 1967 the shareholders saw that the auditors had taken the exceptional step of qualifying the accounts, indicating that they could not judge whether the board's decision to value 'goodwill' so highly in the accounts was wise.

'Much has been said over the years about the auditors qualification,' Goldsmith says today. 'But it was not a question of the auditors being happy or unhappy about the board's decision. There are qualifications every year to the accounts of many leading companies in Britain. The qualification in the Cavenham accounts was because there was a figure for goodwill in the balance sheet, because we paid a premium over net assets for Procea. As the Group was not making money, it was difficult to assess the value of goodwill. Auditors look to the past and not to the future. We thought the company would become profitable – which it did.'

Once again, however, some influential members of the City of London were convinced that their suspicions were true that Cavenham was a company with a rocky past and an uncertain future. The 'qualification' was to become a subject of considerable speculation in the years to come.

'The auditors had to rely on the facts,' he says. 'They could not value one way or the other the goodwill of a company which had not made a profit in the previous year, so all they said in their qualification was that they could not value the goodwill. They neither agreed, nor disagreed, but much propaganda was made about it in subsequent years.'

Undeterred, he issued an interim report to his shareholders, stating firmly, 'For the 52 weeks ended 1st April 1967 Cavenham made a trading loss, including reorganization expenditure, of £947,000,' but 'the results for the first 32 weeks of the current year demonstrate that the reorganization has to a large measure been completed and is beginning to produce the desired effects.' Cavenham had survived, regardless of what anyone might say, but it had been a narrow squeak.

For his part, Jimmy Goldsmith had taken to talking to his employees. He developed a habit of eating lunch in the staff canteen of the company's headquarters in Slough, choosing employees at random and sitting down beside them to find out what they thought of the business and how it was going. To the consternation of his senior managers, he would return from the canteen only to bombard them with memos based on what he had been told, and asking what they intended to do about it. He did not believe in taking a detailed interest in any of his companies, but he adopted a policy which his managers came to call 'creative nosiness'. Over the years he refined this technique until every executive who worked for him knew that they would first learn about his interest from a long inquisitive memo rather than from any more personal contact.

The most successful division of Cavenham at this time was Dietary Foods, which consisted of Procea, Slimcea and Nutrex slimming breads and made up over half the £20 million market in Britain for low-calorie bread, even though Cavenham itself did not bake the bread but merely supplied ingredients to bakers. Indeed, in the space of three years the division's profits rose from £50,000 to £500,000. But even that was not enough to get Cavenham back on its feet. In the summer of 1968, therefore, Jimmy Goldsmith took the only logical step he could. He decided to sell what had proved to be a troublesome acquisition – Singleton and Cole.

In the words of his annual report, 'Our investment in wholesaling of approximately £2·1 million, or about half our capital and reserves, was not profitable.' He went on to blame their difficulties on the Labour Government's policies and added by way of explanation, 'the industry itself was becoming progressively more difficult as a result of increased Selective Employment Tax, the deliberate squeezing of distributive margins as recommended by the Prices and Incomes Board; and the ending of resale price maintenance in both confectionery and tobacco.'

The sale of Singleton and Cole brought Cavenham back into the black, its assets exceeding its liabilities by more than one and a half million pounds. The delicate question of the qualification of the accounts for the second year remained unanswered in the City's mind, however, for the value of the 'goodwill' attached to their purchase of Procea still could not be judged. No matter how sound the group's prospects may have looked, things still did not seem entirely right to everyone about this fast-growing food company. But Goldsmith could not have cared less what the City establishment thought, he was planning his next move.

From the sale of Singleton and Cole he had salvaged two assets that were to prove vital to the development of Cavenham. The first was a snuff-making company, which sold Singleton's and Illingworth's snuffs and which Jim Slater later described as 'the jewel in its crown' which he had 'virtually overlooked'. The second was a tiny chain of twenty-two newsagent's and tobacconist's and sweet shops in Liverpool and Sheffield and trading under the name of Hayes Lyon and run by a former Co-op manager, Jim Wood. The snuff-making company had already taken Cavenham into partnership with the Conwood Corporation, a partnership which was to steadily expand, while the twenty-two shops now took Cavenham into what would eventually become the largest section of its business: retailing.

Never keen to overlook an opportunity, however small, he bought a further sixty shops, the Alex group in London, from the official receiver (after their owner had committed suicide), to expand his retailing division. After selling eleven of them to recoup the money he had paid to buy them, he now boasted a chain of seventy-one shops, which he had acquired at virtually no cost. Small and unfashionable they might be, but within a few months the shops were contributing a steady, regular profit to Cavenham, and what was more important, bringing the company a regular supply of hard cash. For while a manufacturing company had to wait for its customers to pay their bills, the shopkeeper took his money over the counter and kept his suppliers waiting for their money. For a man with an appetite for using any money he could lay his hands on that was a substantial attraction of Cavenham's newly formed Retail Division. Six years after leaving Selim Zilkha to the Lewis and Burrows chain, Goldsmith found himself back in retailing.

As he noted in the company's annual report for 1967/8, 'Since 1965 the Group has paid an average of £170,000 per annum in bank interest and other financial charges,' but as a result of the sale of the wholesaling arm under Singleton and Cole, 'Cavenham Foods, as at present constituted, will no longer normally be a borrower.' By the following year the alarums and excursions of the first three years of Cavenham were well and truly over. The troublesome confectionary division had been sold to the joint Swiss company Conwood S A at a profit, after the deal with Perrier had been unravelled.

Cavenham now rested comfortably on three principal legs: its slimming foods; its groceries, including Carr's water biscuits; and its shops. He said in his annual report as chairman, 'Your company is now ready to expand both by internal growth and by acquisition.' It had achieved the reorganization begun in August 1965, had a 50 per cent share in Conwood S A and cash in the bank. With a flourish he prophesied a profit of £650,000, and Cavenham's shares immediately rose in value on the stock market.

In Britain Jimmy Goldsmith was moving towards manufacturing, and then on to retailing, but in Europe he was becoming a banker. Gustin Milical company continued its profitable path, and in 1968 he and Alexis de Gunzburg had taken over the Union de Participations, formerly an Algerian tram company, and used it as the basis of their development into banking, partly on the advice of one of their friends, John Burton Tigrett, negotiator for Dr Armand Hammer's Occidental Petroleum.

In 1968 they had bought the small Van Embden bank in Amsterdam, and then arranged to buy the Société Générale Foncière which included a Paris bank. After finding partners in the Union Bank of Los Angeles and the Central National Bank of Cleveland (who took 10 per cent each), Jimmy Goldsmith and Alexis de Gunzburg then transformed their former Algerian tram company into Société Générale Occidentale, and named their new French bank, Banque Occidentale.

Once again Jimmy Goldsmith came across a particularly valuable asset in a take-over, although this time it was not in the shape of a chain of shops or a snuff maker; it was a small, demurely dressed French woman who spoke rather slowly and wore her hair tied back in a bun like a music teacher. She was called Madame Gilberte Beaux. In the next few years she was to become his single closest business adviser, the most important individual in his organization.

Then aged thirty-seven Madame Beaux had already been described as the 'best banker in France'. For a girl who had left school in France with no formal qualifications, who had started in banking as a typist at the Seligman Bank in Paris in 1946, this was a remarkable tribute. When only twenty-three, she had become one of Seligman's administrators, and in the same year won a diploma in banking. Married to a half-Russian chemist in the perfumery industry fourteen years her senior, she had a daughter; but her passion was business. In the next four years, she, within Générale Occidentale, became responsible for every aspect of Goldsmith's business interests, as well as his counsellor, alter ego and friend; the person above any other who could restrain his wilder flights of commercial or financial fantasy. He, in return, was to make her rich beyond the dreams of her childhood.

In one area of his life in France, however, matters had not gone so smoothly – the family hotel business. In February 1967 the courteous and gentlemanly Major Frank Goldsmith died. In its obituary *The Times* in London commented, 'Monsieur le Major, as he was always known, was probably the leading figure in the French hotel world in the inter-war years, and certainly the most popular.' He was eighty-eight. His death affected his son deeply. Jimmy Goldsmith was very conscious of his father's love of England, and of his broken hopes for a career in that country.

After the Major's death, the Société des Hôtels Réunis, now under the chairmanship of one of his father's friends, the uncle of the future president of France, Valéry Giscard d'Estaing, tried hard to prevent the aggressive younger son of their old colleague from joining the Board of Directors. 'Monsieur le Major' had not only spent his own inheritance over the years (his brother Teddy had left £106,000 when he died in 1950), he had also quietly sold off shares in the hotel company to his fellow directors when he had needed a little extra money. It hardly made his son's attempts to join the board any easier.

Their attitude not only annoyed Jimmy Goldsmith, it also made him more determined than ever to become a director of the company which his father had helped to create. So when the Hôtel Réunis board wanted to finance its purchase of the freehold of the Carlton Hotel in Cannes (it had until then owned only the lease) and went to the stock market to raise the money, he seized his opportunity. He bought as many shares in the group as he could until the size of his shareholding made it impossible for the directors to do anything but invite him to join their board.

The tactic did not endear him to them, especially as he then proceeded to use every opportunity at board meetings to advocate a policy of rapid expansion and turn the group into one of the most important in Europe. Unimpressed, they firmly rejected his new approach. Finally, desperate to induce some change, he offered each of his fellow directors the opportunity either to buy his shares or sell him theirs at a fixed price, and he gave them two weeks to consider the proposal. After the fortnight had elapsed he asked each one if he had decided to buy or to sell. Each of them refused to do either. So he began discussions with Max Joseph about selling the group to Grand Metropolitan Hotels. About that, at least, everyone was agreed; and it was the only way of breaking the miserable stalemate.

In the meantime his mother and his brother, whose few experiments in business had not proved enormously successful, had decided their best hope of a secure financial future rested with him, and they invested with him their small inheritance from 'Monsieur le Major' and their hotel shares. From now on he would carry the financial hopes of the entire family – which suited him admirably. He had seen himself for some time as the leader of the tribe, and this was formal acknowledgement of the fact. It would be he who would decide what investments should be used,

which houses should be rented, for it was he who had the
financial acumen to do it in the best interests of them all.
In England he was about to prove that they had made a
wise choice.

Jimmy Goldsmith was about to bring off the most spectacular success of his rise to power with Cavenham. Within
three months of acquiring the Birrell and R. S. McColl
chains of 430 shops, from his merchant bankers Keyser
Ullman in March 1971, he had amalgamated them with
his existing chain of 71 newsagent's, tobacconist's and
sweet shops, Hayes Lyon and Alex, and sold off 105 un-
profitable ones. Only six months later proceeded to sell half
the entire chain to the Southland Corporation of Dallas
in Texas for £3·3 million. He had paid less than £1·1 million for them over the past three years. He even negotiated
that the price could rise by up to 20 per cent if they showed
annual profits of more than £375,000 after tax. They did,
and later he did indeed go back to collect his increased
price.
     That deal with the Southland Corporation provided the
launching pad for the take-over which would transform
him from being an industrialist with a slightly eccentric
group of food manufacturing companies into one of the
most formidable financial figures in British industry. He
now launched what he later described as a 'cheeky' bid for
the giant Bovril group of companies. In June 1971 he
offered £9·7 million for it, the following month he raised
his bid to £10·6 million, and in August to £14·5 million;
all the time competing against the vast Rowntree
Macintosh company, which had been invited into Bovril
to save them and were the City of London's clear favour-
ites to win the battle. Disregarding any opposition, he stole
the company from under Rowntree's nose, partly by agreeing to pay rather too much for it.
     At a stroke he had taken over three of the staple
ingredients of almost every British pantry, Bovril, Marmite
and Ambrosia Creamed Rice. As with so many other
acquisitions in Cavenham's history, he had masterminded
this one himself, and within six months he had sold off
parts of the Bovril company's diverse assets (including

their bulk milk business and a *hacienda* in South America) for nearly £7 million, thereby effectively cutting the purchase price in half. Within six months his management team had increased Bovril's profit from some £1·2 million to an estimated £2·2 million a year.

The whole operation suddenly earned him an almost mystical reputation for financial wizardry, yet its speed, coupled with his apparent determination never to stand still, did not entirely dispel the impression that the success was somehow transient, achieved by sleight of hand rather than financial acumen. Nevertheless, he had become a man whose actions were from now on followed and monitored carefully. Despite whispers about a certain lack of judgement, of moving too quickly, he was now a figure to be treated with some respect. The City's grudging accolade gave him a small twinge of pride, but he was determined to capture the City's most carefully protected castles. They had not seen anything yet. As he told an astonished group of his managers at a lunch at the Savoy Hotel in September, almost before the ink was dry on the Bovril take-over, 'We must get on with another acquisition. This bull market is not going to last forever. We must be quick.'

7. Britain's Number One Grocer

In the next two years no one in Jimmy Goldsmith's employment, least of all he himself, had time to pause for breath. He rushed pell-mell through the stock markets of England and France, buying and selling companies like a man moving counters on the backgammon board. He hardly waited for the dice to stop rolling before he moved again. His dream of creating a major European food company, and a rival to Unilever and Nestlé, obsessed him with an intensity that terrified some people and mystified others. His urge to dominate everything and everyone he came into contact with reminded those who watched him of another, fictional, businessman who seemed possessed by the same demon, Charles Foster Kane.

In the scramble for financial power women were his relaxation, his only true hobby. Certainly he gambled regularly, as he had been concentrating on making himself the best backgammon player among his friends, but that was a distraction rather than a pleasure. Beautiful women were his passion.

While he had been sweeping up the ragbag of companies that became Cavenham Foods, Lady Annabel Birley had grown more and more conscious that her marriage was disintegrating. Although her husband knew about her affair he remained devoted to her and, anxious to keep her family together, at least while the children were young, she steadfastly took holidays with her children and her husband. But by 1968 it had become clear that some sort of formal separation was inevitable. As the year progressed, Mark Birley quietly moved out of their home, Pelham Cottage in South Kensington, London, and moved round the corner to Pelham Street. His garden backed on to his family's and the children still saw as much of him as they had done before, but the change in Annabel Birley's life was now marked. During the school terms she would sometimes go away with Jimmy Goldsmith, perhaps to

Marrakesh in the winter, or to the West Indies, but for the rest of the time her children remained her chief concern.

Children were also in Goldsmith's mind. He remained as devoted to his eldest daughter Isabel, who was by now fourteen and living with his wife Ginette in Paris, as he did to his son Manes and daughter Alix. He would spoil them, always arriving for weekends and holidays with presents, usually bringing the unexpected. But he was more like an eternally generous uncle, the man who provided the speedboat or the sledge on holiday, than the bringer of a daily intimacy which most fathers make their own. Some might have interpreted his generosity as guilt, but that would have been a mistake. It was the approach of a man who felt uneasy at most ordinary human relationships, and covered the unease as best he could, with generosity and charm.

He made no secret of his unconventional life. He explained to both Ginette and Annabel Birley that he was a man who had always lived his life in compartments, and that there was little chance he would change now; but that he was devoted to them both. It was an honest, if slightly vain statement, but one he has never altered. Indeed, on one occasion he arranged that both families took their holidays in Sardinia together, and he divided his time between them both, driven from one to the other in his speedboat.

But his life had become obsessed with his financial empire, and the creation of a permanent memorial to the Goldsmith name. The fierce pursuit of commercial success in Europe was his aim. In the five years since Cavenham Foods had struggled off the ground in England, he had also been reorganizing his companies in France and gradually spreading his tentacles into the still developing European Common Market. Indeed in February 1970 Cavenham had announced it was acquiring 60 per cent of a French public company, Financière et Industrielle de Petrole et de Pharmacie (known as FIPP), and that Gustin Milical, for so long the cornerstone of his French financial security, would be merged into another company within FIPP called Laboratories Grémy-Longuet. FIPP also bought Cavenham a group of other pharmaceutical products, including one of the staples of the French bathroom, Synthol; as well as a chemical company called Agrifurane, which was France's leading producer of a cereal distillate, Furfurol, used in food refining. They were hardly glamorous acquisitions but their prospects were steady and improving.

Shortly before the acquisition of FIPP, Goldsmith had also bought the Dutch chocolate firm of Ringer's, and he had decided to buy out the other half share of his Swiss Conwood company from his American partners. He had also purchased the Dutch distillers, Melchers, makers of the famous Dutch gin, Olifant; and had acquired the German snuff company, Wittman GmbH. Not all this European activity turned out to be an unqualified success: Ringer's was sold off within nine months with a loss of £57,000, but in most cases the decisions proved sound, perhaps even a little cautious for a man with such a reckless reputation.

So, as he girded his financial reserves to launch his takeover bid for Bovril, he knew that he had not yet created the group he was dreaming of. He may have been claiming sales for Cavenham of £35 million, profits of nearly £2 million, a long way from the £1 million losses in the days of Carr's of Carlisle, but the group was a ragged amalgam rather than a single force in the European marketplace. Undeniably there was the basis of a management team within Cavenham led by a former Procea man, Jack Greenhalgh, as managing director, and Brian Callaway of the grocery division, but no one could call the group's future settled, no matter how optimistic Jimmy Goldsmith tried to make it appear in the pages of their annual report. Some people even regarded it as hanging on by its fingertips. Furthermore, many in the City of London were intensely critical of the elaborate intercompany dealings that seemed to take place within the Cavenham group, and the suspicion grew that these concealed a less healthy financial picture than that painted by their flamboyant chairman. Jimmy Goldsmith was rather shocked by the unexpected hostility, but he refused to admit that he could possibly have encouraged it, and failed to understand that his flamboyant – some even said overbearing – approach might not appeal to every Englishman, financier or not. It was some years before he finally admitted, 'I am too French in England, and too English in France to be quite at home in either country.'

Nevertheless he was proud that by his own efforts he had created a business and financial group which allowed him absolute freedom of manoeuvre, the right to do as he pleased and to negotiate with whom he chose. He needed to consult no one about his plans – though he tended to take the precaution of discussing them with Madame Beaux in Paris – and he was free to do whatever deal he could. There was no massive board of directors to beware of, for his companies relied principally upon his own energy, determination and ability to seize whatever opportunities presented themselves. Cavenham was a group of companies fashioned in the image of one man, their chairman, whose future would be determined by that one man; and his instincts were essential to its survival.

These instincts were not simply those of a gambler, however, no matter what some sceptical observers of his progress might have believed. His detractors did not wish to hear that he was a voracious reader of detailed analyses of his business prospects, nor did his supporters wish to know that his buccaneering image was equally at fault. Both needed the romantic myths to continue. It made English business that bit more exciting than it might otherwise have been. For his part, Jimmy Goldsmith did not bother to contradict them: if some said he had built a group with a gambler's luck and that he could only have done it so quickly with exceptional drive, let them. After all they did not have to buy his shares, or he theirs.

As Richard Milner pointed out in the *Sunday Times* just before the result of Goldsmith's bid for Bovril was known, 'This, then, has been the rise of James Michael Goldsmith, a fast-moving entrepreneur who has chanced his arm and won more often than he has lost. His methods have not always been orthodox, nor has he always lived up to his own expectations ... Bovril shareholders considering the Cavenham offer must assess the risks and rewards offered by this remarkable man, who combines the talents of a financial Houdini and a commercial Master Builder.'

The 'Master Builder' had come to believe he had

enemies, however, and among them not just cautious financiers in the City of London, but also some financial journalists who, he believed, were inspired by his commercial rivals. Despite the confident appearance presented to the financial community, he had began to suspect that there were some who were deliberately conspiring against him. This suspicion was fuelled over the ensuing years by an increasing conviction that he was the victim of an organized attempt to detract from his success and force him back into obscurity. The feeling seemed to light a tiny flame of paranoia that appeared to become a central part of his character, the other side of his eternal confidence. Neither could exist without the other, and they have been handmaidens throughout his career ever since.

In France, however, he felt far less haunted by his critics. There he felt comfortable, aware that his was a European attitude to life, and that few, if any, would decry it. He felt that in England he had enemies, whereas in France there were simply some who did not agree with him; and he had no objection to that. So, inevitably, it was in France that he had chosen to establish the basis of his company in 1970, when he had effectively pushed Cavenham inside the French firm, FIPP. That in turn was to be controlled by the Generale Occidentale company which he and Alexis de Gunzburg had created from the Algerian Tramway company. It also took under its wing his newly acquired banking operations in Amsterdam, in Paris with the Banque Occidentale, and, finally, in Vienna with the Centrofin bank which had been formed in partnership with the London bank Kleinwort Benson and the communist Bank Handlowy. GO, as the French company was universally known, became the ultimate holding company of all his operations throughout Europe, GO allowed itself relatively little independent movement in its first years, beyond buying nearly 24 per cent of the Eiffel Tower which proved a speculative investment as Goldsmith failed to persuade the Tower's board of directors to expand their enterprises, much as he had failed to persuade the directors of his father's hotel company a few years before. He decided there were quite enough businessmen who were prepared to accept his ideas and his appetite for speed for him not to waste time on those that did not. GO sold its shareholding within a year, and it convinced him to do business with single entrepreneurs like himself rather than large boards of directors, it was a preference he has never lost.

Even though in England the Cavenham Food group, which changed its name to Cavenham in August 1971 because of its interests outside food, was the proud boast of its chairman, then still only thirty-eight, not everyone was convinced. As the *Financial Times* commented, his group was 'widely regarded as a nonentity in the food business, and at best a speculative stock ... slimming breads, some confectionery, a few biscuits, Dutch gin, snuff and a relatively modest chain of confectionery, newspaper and tobacconists shops hardly add up to a major force in the market place. It was a far cry from the Cadbury Schweppes and Rank Hovis MacDougall league.' Yet they were forced to admit, barely six months later, that 'today Cavenham is undoubtedly in that league'.

For in the last few months of 1971 Jimmy Goldsmith mounted his final assault on the commanding heights of British business, and in a few months transformed his group from a small ragbag of companies with a turnover of £35 million a year to among the largest food groups in Europe with sales of £400 million a year.

The sale of half Cavenham's newly enlarged retail division of 360 shops to the American Southland Corporation of Dallas, Texas, had brought in the large sum of £3·3 million: their first major victory was the acquisition of Bovril. He had paid more than some City observers thought the company was properly worth, but he had confounded those who believed he never had a chance. As the *Financial Times* commented, 'Some people are still shaking their heads in disbelief.'

In September 1971 he launched two bids: one for the Wright's biscuit-making firm, which had sales of £24 million, and the other for the Moore's group of more than 1000 grocery shops with sales of £51·9 million. He offered £10 million for both companies, and got them. In November he sold Bovril's bulk milk supplying business to the Express Dairy for £4·7 million, but that was a mere tidying-up operation; the next major assault was already being planned.

He wanted to take over the fourth largest chain of grocery shops in Britain, Allied Suppliers, right under the noses of the major grocery chains, including Tesco and Sainsbury's. And he planned to do it from the hardly inspiring base of owning 360 newsagent's and 760 newly acquired grocery shops which had until recently been losing about a million pounds a year. The owner of a ragamuffin collection of shops had set his sights on some of the best known names in Britain's High Streets, including Lipton's, the Home and Colonial, and Maypole Dairies. His target also had the attraction of being one of the blue-chip companies whose share price made up the *Financial Times* 30 share index, which provided the guide to stock market movements. It was at the very heart of the British financial establishment.

The size of his bid shocked even the already dazzled City. It was the largest he had yet launched. In January 1972 he announced his intention to bid £82·5 million for the giant company with its sales of almost £270 million a year. Within a week he had raised his bid to £86·3 million. His friend Jim Slater had told him that unless he succeeded with his bid for Bovril he would never be able to launch another take-over in the City, and he now intended testing if this were true. He had succeeded once, he could do so again.

Jimmy Goldsmith had learned that the best way of entering an institution you wanted to take over was to make sure someone was prepared to open the door to let you in. Before launching the takeover bid he had therefore quietly arranged to buy the 12 per cent of Allied Supplier's shares held by his potential rival, Unilever. In return he agreed to sell Allied Supplier's tea interests to Unilever when he took over. The vital 12 per cent gave him a third of Allied's voting rights and, and by a quick increase in the offer price for Allied Supplier's shares, he also got the company's board of directors' support. So by the middle of January 1972 he controlled Allied Suppliers, a constituent of the FT index and a blue-chip company. The

City of London could never again dismiss him as an upstart who was going to cut and run.

At a stroke Cavenham's sales had become £400 million a year, its share price had gone up from 90 pence to 229 pence in six months, and it now employed some 75,000 people. It was the fastest, most spectacular piece of financial and industrial empire-building the City of London had seen for a decade; and it was accomplished almost exactly ten years to the day after he had been forced to sell his share in the embryonic Mothercare chain. Less than eight years had passed since his first stake in Carson's chocolate, and only just over six years since the creation of the Cavenham group from Carr's of Carlisle and the rest of the mixed bag of sweets, sugar mice and biscuits.

The *Daily Mirror* called him 'Britain's Number One Grocer'. The *Observer* said he was 'the financier with the golden touch', and almost every other British newspaper called him the City's new 'whizzkid'. But there were one or two who were not quite so impressed. The *Financial Times* reported, 'The argument runs thus: if the events of the past few months have materially increased Jimmy Goldsmith's reputation for financial wizardry – a reputation which has not always brought him universal approval – they have so far done little to prove that he can actually run the empire of his dreams.

'The new group is on a different scale altogether from the old Cavenham: and so are the problems that he has bought himself. Does Cavenham have either the top management or the experience to be able to cope?'

It was a question that had not crossed his mind. He never questioned that his management had the ability to cope. They had coped so far; and he had never interested himself in the details of any of his individual companies since the early days of his forays into the canteen. He preferred to leave the administration of the companies to his division's managers, and to pay them handsomely to make their own decisions. In his time as the owner of Bovril he had hardly set foot in a factory, he simply knew it was there from the balance sheet and the monthly returns he received. Besides, he did not see himself as the manager of his empire; he was its architect. Like Napoleon, he wanted his generals to run it. He would create the strategy, and they would execute it.

So as his management began to see if they could actually control the Leviathan he had created for them, he set out to raise it some cash. He proceeded to sell for £18·5 million the tea interests of Allied Suppliers to Unilever, as he had agreed before the take-over; and he began to look seriously at their property interests with a view to raising another £20 million. He even considered selling half the new retail shops to the Southland Corporation of Dallas, and thereby raise himself another £25 million or more, but they decided that was more than they could afford, so he did not.

Nevertheless, by 1972 Goldsmith was no longer simply a businessman on the rise, he was well on the way to becoming one of the richest men in Europe. He had built the third largest food manufacturing group in Europe. One person in every twelve in Britain either bought their groceries from him, or ate his products. In spite of his buccaneering style, he had not created his group out of unheard-of companies. Throughout he had maintained a distinctly cautious approach by buying well established brand names, wherever he could, and developing their potential rapidly by cutting back on wide-ranging research projects in favour of specific ones, and public relations budgets in favour of strengthening the marketing department and his management's hand by giving them bigger budgets to do the essential job of selling the brands they were responsible for. Above all, he had invested in products that would always be necessary, the staples of life. Demand for them would remain when recession made luxuries less certain investments. It was a philosophy he has continued to hold, no matter how often encouraged by his contemporaries to be more daring. He shied away from buying much property, in spite of the property boom.

Six years earlier he had excitedly told Jim Slater, while pacing up and down the Slater Walker offices in Hertford Street, 'the main problem is the ecological one.' Utterly bewildered, Slater asked him what he was talking about. Goldsmith had explained, 'Before long there will be a shortage of water; in America the crime rate is rising at over 30 per cent per annum; within five years you will not be able to get fish from the sea; there will be a shortage of food . . .' The ideas may have been exaggerated, perhaps inspired in him by his brother's growing interests in ecology, but they nevertheless had their impact on his strategy as a businessman.

But still he did not stop running. In July 1972 he disposed of the company that had got Cavenham on the road in the first place, Carr's of Carlisle. It was sold together with the biscuit interests of Wright's and Kemp's Biscuits to the giant United Biscuit Company for £4 million in cash. Then in August he sold his friend Jim Slater nearly £4 million-worth of Allied Supplier's property for £4 million in cash.

Goldsmith also kept up the pace in France. In January 1972, while he was completing the Allied deal in England he was buying the Sanders company, which produced pharmaceuticals and animal foods in France, Belgium and Spain, and the Sodep company doing a similar thing in Luxembourg. In May he bought 20 per cent of the giant Générale Alimentaire food group, with a view to merging it with his existing FIPP thus creating one of France's leading companies. But as he did so he was further refining his objectives. The desire to gain control and power was subtly undergoing a transformation. As he put it in his chairman's statement for Cavenham in October 1972, 'I think it would be useful to restate our policy with regard to investment in Europe, outside the UK. We believe that companies, if they are significant, should form part of the community in which they are based. National pride is a fact of life which can be a powerful asset in developing any major enterprise. We would think it wrong to inhibit the driving force by attempting to run overseas companies from London, or even to seek total ownership.'

It was the first significant sign that he might have had ambitions larger than simply becoming a food tycoon. It seemed to imply that his ideas had gained a political dimension, which was strengthened as he went on to argue in the same chairman's report, 'Our policy is therefore where possible to participate in Europe as a major shareholder rather than as an outright owner; it is to back national management with our capital, our technology and our methods of management and to make available our strong international commercial organization. This already consists of Europe's largest food retailing group ... in this way we can work in full sympathy with national authorities; we can attract the most able management talent; we can have as partners local institutions and the public; and we can compete with locally owned companies on equal terms.'

As 1972 drew to a close, he controlled some of the most important groceries and brand new names in Europe, and many of the shops that sold them. In England his companies owned Slimcea and Procea, Carson's liqueur chocolates, Elizabeth Shaw Mint Crisps, Parkinson's boiled sweets, Holland's toffees, Illingworth's snuffs, Bovril, Marmite and Ambrosia. All these products were sold in a chain of nearly 2500 shops called everything from Liptons to Maypole. In France he still had Milical and the pharmaceutical companies; but he now also owned Anders, producing animal food concentrates with an annual turnover of £40 million, not to mention Générale Alimentaire's food brands, including Amora with half the mustard market, Dessaux with about half the vinegar market, Vandamme spiced cake and Aussage spices and peppers with between 25 and 40 per cent of their respective markets. He owned the profitable snuff business Wittman in Germany, Melcher's Olifant gin in Holland; and 25 per cent of the Danish Irma chain of food shops. All these were simply Cavenham interests. Générale Occidentale's European banking arms stretched above them.

By September 1972 even the previously sceptical *Sunday Times* was acknowledging that Générale Occidentale was the centre of his European financial empire. 'Through this he controls the whole of his proliferating Europe-wide empire, now valued by the Stock Market at over £200 million.' Certainly it was GO, as it was known by Goldsmith's French shareholders, which also oversaw his investment and banking subsidiary, Anglo-Continental Investments, begun only nine months earlier, which had expanded rapidly during the nine months in which Cavenham was digesting Allied Suppliers and Générale Alimentaire.

Anglo-Continental was hardly a surprise, however, as it primarily represented a number of deals he had quietly gone into with his old backgammon opponent, Jim Slater. By this time the two men were having dinner once a fortnight, usually at Wilton's in London's Bury Street, a restaurant of which the late Major Frank Goldsmith had always been fond. Indeed it was at one of these dinners in July 1972 that the first of the Slater/Goldsmith deals was struck. Anglo-Continental bought two of Jim Slater's satellite companies, Thomas Stevens and Tanker Investment Trust for £9 million and £8 million respectively, and he also agreed to take over effective control of Jim Slater's property company, Argyle Securities, by taking a third of its equity. In return Jim Slater got 10 per cent of Anglo-Continental. The details were worked out on the back of a waiter's order pad in Wilton's. As Slater remembered in his autobiography, *Return to Go*, 'Slater Walker ended up with three satellites less, a lot of cash and a few Anglo-Continental shares; whereas Jimmy had very substantially boosted the underlying asset value of Anglo-Continental by issuing its shares for relatively hard assets.' Slater, as he himself explained, had realized he would have to sell whole companies if he intended to move into cash as he said he did.

A month later, again in Wilton's, with his friend eating caviar at his customary electric speed, Jim Slater did another deal with him, this time for £43 million and again worked out on a waiter's pad. This time Anglo-Continental acquired the insurance brokers Wigham Richardson and two of Slater's investment trusts, Flag and Irish. The two men could not agree on the price to be paid, and decided to play for whether it should be £42 or £43 million. Goldsmith won choice of game and chose backgammon, at which he was now among the best half-dozen players in Britain. He won, and got the trusts for £1 million less than Slater had envisaged. Ironically, had Jim Slater won choice of game and opted for chess, he would almost certainly have won; Jimmy Goldsmith's passion for speed made chess á game in which he took no pleasure – the results were too long in arriving.

For a time, at least, Anglo-Continental was a significant

part of his empire. It controlled the Slater companies, including Argyle Securities, plus the Dutch van Embden Bank (now renamed the Occidentale Bank) as well as a Swiss Bank, Ralli Brothers.

The fact that his empire had a French base had escaped the notice of almost every observer of Cavenham's rapid developments during the first two years of the 1970s. Hypnotized by the speed and size of his acquisitions in England, the watchers in the City of London overlooked the significant detail that he had delicately pushed Cavenham into GO in 1970. Indeed, it was September before most people began to realize that England was not his entire ambition. As the *Sunday Times* reported in 1972, 'Many people have suspected that there must be a mysterious French financier behind Jimmy Goldsmith and his fast moving London companies, Cavenham and the Anglo-Continental banking octopus. There is. But it is Goldsmith himself, wearing another hat, sitting above the Champs Elysee in the modest offices of a virtually unknown operation called Générale Occidentale ... Through this he controls the whole of his proliferating Europe wide empire now valued by the Stock Market at over £200 million.'

As he told *Sunday Times* reporter James Poole, 'If there is one thing I wish I had done with Générale Occidentale ... I wish I had kept it private.' It was the sentiment of a man who liked to work in secret. That way he could dictate to it in his own way.

In September 1972, a week after the terrorists had disrupted the Olympic Games in Munich, Goldsmith, along with seven other European businessmen, including his friend Jim Slater, appeared on the cover of *Time* magazine as one of eight new young European businessmen who were making their influence felt from Iberia to Scandinavia. 'Multi-national in their attitudes, multi-lingual and young, they are quietly changing the style and stepping up the pace of European business,' the magazine said.

Jimmy Goldsmith 'is a true multi-national man ... who claims to have learned the art of management from the mistakes of US multi-nationals,' *Time* went on breathlessly. 'Almost to a man the managers who are coming to the forefront in Europe have a dominant objective, they

Madame Marcelle Goldsmith
outside the Carlton in Cannes,
one of the most splendid of
Major Frank Goldsmith's many
hotels

Frank Goldsmith MP ('Monsieur le
Major')

The Goldsmith family in 1936: (*standing, left to right*) Georgilia (wife
of Edward), Ernst von Marx (husband of Nelly), Frank, Nelly
(aunt), Edward (uncle), Teddy (brother); (*sitting, left to right*)
Jimmy, Marcelle, Boma von Marx (cousin)

Jimmy Goldsmith (*left*) and his brother Teddy

Jimmy Goldsmith aged six

Yet another front-page news story about the elopement of Jimmy Goldsmith and Isabel Patino (*Syndication International*)

Daily Mirror

FORWARD WITH THE PEOPLE

The wedding today is off, but—

THE RUNAWAY LOVERS REMAIN IN HIDING

NOW BRITISH RAILWAYS PRESENT THE BILL

'DAILY MIRROR' REPORTERS,
Edinburgh, Tuesday

SOMEWHERE in Scotland tonight Isabella Patino, the singing heiress, and James Goldsmith, the man she loves, were wondering what to do next after the legal ban imposed on their marriage at noon tomorrow.

And in his Edinburgh hotel suite Isabella's father, Bolivian

A Goldsmith stag party

After their marriage. Isabel Goldsmith is wearing the outfit in which she had escaped from Paris two weeks earlier and had worn ever since (*Topham*)

Jimmy Goldsmith with his first daughter Isabel in September 1954 after he had won the right to her custody (*Topham*)

Jimmy Goldsmith and Ginette Lery, who later became his second wife, three years after the birth of their son Manes (*Topham*)

Jimmy Goldsmith's daughter Isabel marries Baron Arnaud de Rosnay in Paris, June 1973 (*Syndication International*)

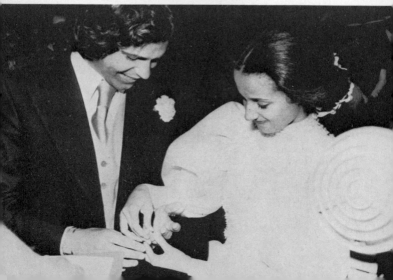

are reaching out for new markets.' For the vast uncommitted majority, the metamorphosis of the playboy into the financier was complete.

As 1972 drew to a close Jimmy Goldsmith realized that the first half of his life was over. He would be 40 in a matter of weeks, but he looked back over the past two years with some pride, even a little vanity. Using a mixture of strategy, opportunism, financial expertise, determination, guile and force of personality, he had created a giant grocery chain with a turnover of £450 million a year and 3000 shops – the biggest in Europe – as well as a banking group valued at more than £60 million. In the past half century few other industrialists or financiers had achieved so much so quickly, and few others would not then have decided to relax.

But to a man whose confident exterior concealed the fear that everything that has been achieved can just as quickly return to dust, there could be no standing still. He knew that there had to be more change, still more expansion. That way lay an active mind, one which had no time to dwell on what might go wrong. That way the demons could be kept at bay. That way, he told himself, the future could be permanently assured. While he was deciding on the appropriate move he would do what he usually did when there was a lull at the beginning of the year, he would throw a party. After all, his daughter Isabel deserved something to mark her eighteenth birthday last year. A party was the obvious thing, especially if it was one which no one could possibly forget.

8. A Party in Acapulco

In all the sixty-seven distinguished years of its history, the Ritz Hotel had seldom seen such a fuss for a party, or such extravagance. In the magnificent mirrored rooms of its basement a team of florists were painstakingly removing every single one of the hotel's own decorations and replacing them with orchids and palms. Designers and stage hands were anxiously pulling curtains and pushing music stands to create suitable settings for the five jazz bands which had been specially flown to London from New Orleans to provide the music. It might be the first fortnight of 1973 but for the 250 guests leaving the chill air of Piccadilly that evening the illusion of a summer night in Louisiana had to be complete. Jimmy Goldsmith insisted upon it.

The London 'season', in which the debutante daughters of the English aristocracy 'came out' into society, had ended five years earlier when the official presentations at court had stopped, but it was still possible for a young woman to be launched into society, provided her father was rich enough to do it. Jimmy Goldsmith was certainly rich enough, and his daughter Isabel was unquestionably beautiful enough to have graced any debutante's ball in the previous fifty years.

Perhaps Goldsmith felt a little guilty about his daughter Isabel. Perhaps he knew in his heart that he could have spent more time with her during her childhood, giving her a father's advice and encouragement. Instead, after his battle to decide her future, he had all too often left her alone with her nanny, or at boarding school or with his wife Ginette. He had treated her generously but she remained a slightly neglected figure, a poor little rich girl who knew she could have everything she wanted, except what she wished for most – the love of her own mother.

As the preparation for her 'coming out' party went ahead apace, however, those thoughts were a long way from either

Jimmy or the beautiful young Isabel Goldsmith's mind. He was intent on making it an occasion his guests would remember, she on making sure she did not make a fool of herself. The thought of a room full of people she did not know terrified her. She had not inherited her father's taste for parties, and though she knew how striking she looked she was still frightened out of her wits. She would just have to stern herself to the ordeal. There might just turn out to be someone she could talk to.

With her flowing dark hair, her mother's strong straight nose and fierce eyes, Isabel Goldsmith seemed slightly younger than her eighteen years. Small, with a skin the texture of porcelain, and delicate bones, she could almost have passed for twelve. She had attended a Swiss convent, followed by two years preparing for O levels at a boarding school in Sussex, which she later described as 'horrible!', and then studying for two A levels at the British school in Paris – French, in which she was as bi-lingual as her father, and art. As she was to tell *Vogue* later, 'I wasn't allowed out. I'd never been to a nightclub except for a family outing.' So in spite of her exotic, striking good looks she had remained a shy, slightly withdrawn girl. 'I was forced to come out. I was very very shy.'

But in the basement of the Ritz in London on that January night in 1973 Isabel Goldsmith did her best to play her part as her father would have wished, no matter how hard she found it to talk to guests who, more her father's friends than her own, included Lord Goodman, Lord Lambton, Sir Max Joseph, Lady Melchett and Lady Annabel Birley. There was one guest, however, who did catch her eye. He was a handsome young photographer who told her he had been taking pictures of all sorts of people in Paris, including the actress Marisa Berenson. Tall, with a skier's bumpy nose and slightly reckless look in his eye, the Baron Arnaud de Rosnay was eight years older than Isabel, but he was someone she could talk to. He made her laugh and he seemed to know her father's friends. For someone as keen as she was to curb her shyness, he was a godsend.

After the splendid party for his daughter, Goldsmith began thinking how to celebrate his fortieth birthday in a few weeks' time. Finally he decided. He would take a group of his friends away from the miseries of an English winter and the uncertainty of Phase Two of Edward Heath's government's incomes policy. They could play backgammon, sit in the sun and relax, and the break would give him an opportunity to plan his next steps. It would give him a chance to prepare his mind for the recession that he already suspected would be far worse than anyone anticipated. During the previous summers he had taken his friends to a yacht in the Mediterranean. But this time they would go to Acapulco. Who should he invite? Annabel would be able to come because it was during the school term, and he decided to ask his old associate Peter West, who had done so many things for him over the years, and Dominic Elwes, the painter who was always good company and who was Annabel's second cousin. He might also invite one or two of his gambling friends from the Clermont Club including 'Lucky' Lucan, whom John Aspinall knew rather better than he did, but was usually amusing company. What Jimmy Goldsmith could not know then was that the holiday he was cheerfully planning would eventually come to haunt him, because it would draw him into a series of libel actions destined to make him one of the most publically criticized men in England.

In the villa overlooking the Pacific in February he began to reflect that his life was not quite fulfilled. It did not quite contain everything he wanted. He decided he wanted another, English, family; and he wanted Annabel to have his children. After all, they had been together nine years, her children were growing up, and so were his. In the soft tropical air, with nothing much to occupy his mind, it became a persuasive, insinuating thought.

When he told her, Annabel Birley knew every member of the Londonderry family would object strongly (they had not been entirely happy when her aunt had married his cousin, Lord Jessel); but she also knew she loved him and she liked children. She always had done. Perhaps another child might not be so difficult to cope with. It would be a new interest, something to keep her young.

Jimmy Goldsmith also thought about the future of the companies he had created, and how their range might be extended. He began to wonder if the European markets were quite big enough to allow him to ensure his dreams would not disappear in the cold light of a European recession. In America the prospects seemed so much larger, and the pursuit of profit and commercial gain so much more respectable, less liable to be criticized, than in Europe. Indeed, one or two major British companies had already begun investing in North America. The massive British American Tobacco company, for example, had bought Saks and Gimbel's stores in New York.

In the sunshine of the Mexican winter Jimmy Goldsmith began to develop a fresh strategy for the future beyond simply creating a group to rival Nestlé or Unilever in Europe. The more he travelled in America, the more convinced he became that it was the only place for a company to develop in the last quarter of the century. However there was one further European takeover to launch before a move to the United States was inevitable. He had quietly decided to launch what he called 'Project Grand Slam' to bid for the giant British American Tobacco company, in what would be the biggest takeover bid in British industrial history. When he came back from Acapulco he had a series of secret meetings with Sir John Partridge, the chairman of Imperial Tobacco, who owned 28 per cent of the BAT shares. 'We agreed in principle', Goldsmith said later, 'that Cavenham would buy 14·9 per cent of BAT for cash and the remainder of Imperial's holdings for shares and loan stocks.'

Immediately after that was complete he intended to launch a bid for all the capital of BAT. 'This would have meant that I had created one of the largest international companies, and my plan was that it would have a twinning arrangement between France and Britain, similar to the twin structure of Unilever between the Netherlands and Britain.' It would also have meant that he had achieved his great ambition of that time, 'a major worldwide company engaged in the manufacture and sale of consumer products'. The new company would have been larger than Unilever, 'and firmly anchored in the two countries I considered my own, Britain and France.'

The plan stumbled not because of Goldsmith's lack of

financial acumen, but because Sir John Partridge thought he should inform the then Prime Minister Edward Heath about the plan. 'Ted Heath asked him not to go through with it,' Goldsmith recalls, 'unless it could be a friendly bid. He did not want a massive takeover fight at that time in his government.' Sir John Partridge then decided that he would only go through with his part of the deal, and the sale of Imperial's holdings in BAT to Cavenham, if Goldsmith could convince the board of British American Tobacco to agree to the takeover. Goldsmith met the then chairman of BAT, Sir Richard Dobson, together with some of his colleagues, but, as he was to say later, 'as was inevitable, they did not want to be gobbled up.' It was a dismal end to his grand slam.

So by the end of 1973, Jimmy Goldsmith had reached the conclusion that he must move quietly out of Europe towards America in the next decade. At a time when most people were convinced he was intent on nothing more than dominating the European food industry that might strike some as a very odd conclusion, but he was content to let people think what they liked. He would follow his own strategy. Indeed, his first step, to pull out of the property business into which he had stumbled almost by accident in the past year, had already begun after he got back to England from Acapulco in February 1973. That month he sold two of Allied Suppliers larger buildings in London, in the City Road and in Finsbury Square, although Allied were allowed to stay in City Road, a former Lipton's tea warehouse, for three years. (By a strange twist of fate, five years later Jimmy Goldsmith would find himself back in the building again, as a tenant. It was the site of the offices of his English news magazine *Now!*.) The sale to Cavendish Land company raised £11·7 million in cash.

Over the next few months more than one commentator would suggest that he was foolish to be selling property at a time like this. It was only much later that they realized it was he, and not the companies buying from him, who had done a good deal. As the *Sunday Times* reported two years later, 'He was deep into real estate at the time when inflation made it almost impossible not to make money. But he pulled out of the game still ahead, and waited for other, rasher players to falter. As a result he was able to insulate his own main property vehicle, Argyle Securities, by selling off a string of developments near the peak of the market and using the proceeds to buy and cancel £10·2 million-worth of loan stocks, for only £5·7 million. While others were finding themselves strangled by interest charges which could not be covered by rental earnings, Goldsmith was free and clear.'

In April 1973, however, the sale of his property was replaced in his mind by his daughter Isabel. The photographer whom she had met at the Ritz had encouraged her to overcome her shyness by taking her out as much as possible – at least that was the explanation she had given her father – and now she had decided to marry Baron Arnaud de Rosnay. She was not quite nineteen, and he was twenty-six. She knew that her father had taken a similar decision himself when he was just a year older than she and had decided to elope with her mother. Father and daughter were more alike than either of them cared to admit: for both of them, rebellion came naturally. Not for one moment did Jimmy Goldsmith hesitate. A party had to be held to celebrate the engagement, and the Laurent restaurant near the foot of the Champs Elysée was the obvious place. Arnaud's family, who had been sugar planters in Mauritius, would come and so would Isabel's grandfather, Antenor Patino – the old rift between he and his former son-in-law seemed to have healed. To mark the occasion Arnaud gave Isabel an engagement ring with a Salvador Dali miniature of a swan on a lake set in diamonds. For a wedding present he told her he intended to give her an island of 2400 acres in the Mozambique channel between East Africa and Madagascar.

Jimmy Goldsmith enjoyed his daughter's engagement party. Annabel had come over from London specially, and so had John Aspinall and Dominic Elwes. He also rather liked the gilt mirrored, ornate restaurant and its enthusiastic young staff. Indeed he liked it so much that by midnight he had decided to buy it. He approached the young manager and asked if the owner might be prepared to sell it. The young man felt sure the tall financier was simply showing the effects of the night's champagne, and so he smiled politely and ushered him back towards his own party. No, no, the party's host assured him. This was perfectly serious and he was certainly in a position to buy it. Their conversation wandered on uncertainly until finally, in an effort to see the host back with his guests, the manager agreed to meet him again the next day to discuss it. By that time he felt sure the whole idea would have been forgotten. After all, as far as he was aware, the host had hardly set foot inside the Laurent restaurant before. Why should he suddenly decide to buy it on the strength of a single evening? But he had underestimated the passionate determination of the party's host. The idea did not wear off, the next day's meeting did take place, as did a series of others, and before long Goldsmith had indeed become the proprietor, though not the manager, of the expensively discrete Laurent Restaurant. Ironically it was to be one of the very few businesses he would retain in France after his plan to move to America had been carried out, but that was a long way off. For the moment it was a toy he would not give up, an interest that he could afford. Besides, if you were going to eat out regularly, as he always had done, why not spend the money in your own group.

After Isabel's engagement he returned to his property sales. He sold almost all the remaining surplus shops and offices in the Allied Suppliers', Moore's and Wright's groups to Guardian properties for £17·5 million, of which he was to receive £8·75 million before the end of September. The balance had to be paid before the end of 1976. At the same time he finally disposed of the Bovril companies in Argentina. It was a move which had been under discussion for some time, but had taken a little organizing. In June the final purchase of Générale Alimentaire, the French food manufacturer, was all but completed, bringing the French and English expansion to its end. Générale Alimentaire and Cavenham, under their holding company Générale Occidentale in Paris, were to remain the two principal supports of his empire in Europe for the following six years. Anglo-Continental Investments slowly evaporated. In October 1973 that structure was formally recognized as FIPP began to disappear into GA, along with the Spanish and Belgian company Sanders, Laboratoires Grémy-Longuet and Agrifurane. In the meantime, however, Cavenham in England effectively managed GA in France, and the companies' shareholding was organized to allow them to do so. It was the English company that had the management experience the group needed.

But it was in December 1973 that Goldsmith's musings in Acapulco ten months earlier bore their first fruit; Cavenham, through one of its subsidiary companies, bought control of the American supermarket chain Grand Union for $64 million, of which almost $61 million was raised for them by Hambro's Bank by a Eurodollar loan.

It was a considerable coup. Grand Union employed 27,000 people in its 600 shops, including 531 supermarkets on the east coast of America, and in 1974 it boasted sales of almost $1500 million, which made it the ninth largest food shopping group in the United States. With a swoop typical of his European expansion five years before, he had launched an invasion of America. But times were not as hard as they had been: he was not forced to buy companies on the verge of liquidation; he was not the 'poor man' he had so often described himself as then. In four years Cavenham had expanded from a ragbag group of companies with a turnover of £35 million and profits under £2 million to one with a turnover of £763 million and profits before tax of £31 million.

As he was to put it in his chairman's statement for the year with a distinct touch of pride, 'A recent issue of *Management Today* analyses the results over the past ten years of Britain's leading companies. Cavenham comes out top and by a considerable margin ... We started by acquiring and reorganizing a group of small companies largely in confectionery which for the most part were run down to the point where they would have to be put into liquidation – and which in the process would have put some 2000 people out of employment. We reconstructed this group of companies by strengthening management, closing and selling out-of-date factories, investing the proceeds to modernize other factories, develop new products, and put the companies back on the road to healthy organic growth. It sounds easy but it was not. We almost failed – but we also gained a great deal of experience.'

His invasion of America was not the only part of his Acapulco plan that had come to fruition. Against her family's advice and their sternest warnings, and in spite of the fact that she was still married to Mark, Annabel Birley had decided to have a child with Jimmy Goldsmith. By August she knew she was pregnant, and so did Mark Birley. Once again he offered her the chance to come back to him, but she refused. She knew nothing would change and she had decided on her future. She would stick to it. Some people might be shocked, but she would not let that put her off, the Londonderrys took brave decisions. It was part of the family tradition.

When Annabel Birley gave birth to a daughter, whom they called Jemima, on 30 January 1974 in the Westminster Hospital in London, Jimmy Goldsmith was delighted. A look of boyish pride kept returning to his face as he paced her private room. Some people looked askance at the daughter of a Marquis bearing an illegitimate child of a man who was already married in France, but she did not care, and neither did he. The gossip columns and the sceptical friends could say what they liked, they both loved children and wanted to have them together. He liked the idea of an English family, no matter where his plans for overseas companies might take him, and she liked the idea of having another young family, even though she was thirty-nine. Within three months she was pregnant again.

The stock market in Britain fell steadily as 1973's economic prospects became gloomier and gloomier but Jimmy Goldsmith had reason to feel exultant. His invasion of America had begun, his new family had started, and his predictions about property seemed about to come true. But Jimmy Goldsmith's contentment was not to last.

In the years afterwards there were those who saw 1974 as the first watershed in his career, his first significant failure. The golden touch that seemed to have burnished his business in the past decade evaporated, giving way to a distinctly less fortunate phase, as he extended his interest into politics. His winning streak seemed to be replaced by bitter public criticism and controversy. Some claimed he brought the change upon himself as his increasingly political views – which were followed in turn by a far closer association with politicians – meant that he no longer understood the world he was moving in. It was one thing to be a bright financier on the rise, they were to argue, quite another to enter the arena of active politics. But Goldsmith did not hesitate for a moment. After all the architect of the most successful company in *Management Today*'s survey had a right to a voice in the political debate and he believed, as he had always done, that his opinions were to be taken seriously. There were politicians who would benefit from listening.

Certainly, after his return from Acapulco he had begun to take a much more political attitude to his business. This was very clear in his chairman's statement in the Cavenham annual report.

The statement he had written in June 1973, shortly after his daughter's marriage at St Clothilde, not far from his Paris house near Les Invalides, which had been the scene of his final public reconciliation with Antenor Patino, was brief, and briskly commercial. 'We have disposed of most assets that were incompatible with our objectives as food manufacturers and distributors. Bovril has sold its Argentinian investments in ranching and slaughtering ... Allied Suppliers disposed of much of its surplus property ... Also under our guidance our associated company, Générale Alimentaire, has disposed of the bulk of its activities outside the food industry which it had acquired before we made our investment in the company and as a result of a misguided attempt to diversify,' it remarked in the midst of a description of profits and dividends.

But by August 1974, and his next chairman's statement, the description of his group's achievements had been replaced by elaborate political analysis, couched in grandiose terms, condemning the nature of British society and its reactions to commercial enterprise. After defending the concept of shareholders, Goldsmith went on, 'It is equally easy to attack the profit motive as something socially unacceptable. In fact profits are the lifeblood of industry that enable it constantly to renew and improve itself. Profits are used essentially for three purposes: over half goes in the form of tax and so is ploughed back into the community; a minority of what remains goes as dividend on the capital invested – and to the extent that institutions are shareholders this represents the income which is again ploughed back into the community as pension and insurance payments and as further investments in industry; the final slice is reinvested in the company to help it grow and remain competitive.' He concluded fiercely, 'The only real solution is for British industry to get the capital it needs through sane and realistic attitudes to profit; otherwise vital investment will be curtailed and this will inevitably lead to inefficiency and decrepitude.' It was an altogether new public tone, and some people, both within Cavenham and outside it, wondered what had brought it about.

The answer was straightforward enough. Jimmy Goldsmith had recognized that being the chairman of a successful company in Britain in 1974 brought the responsibility to speak in what he was to call the 'public debate', and he saw no reason to avoid using the opportunity. After all, in the past few years he had reached a number of conclusions about society.

Perhaps like some of his other enthusiasms over the years his new appetite for sweeping political generalization had been nurtured by his elder brother Teddy Goldsmith. For Teddy had remained very close to his younger, more successful brother. Indeed late in 1970 Jimmy had helped Teddy launch the Ecological Foundation, and Teddy had gone on to found the *Ecologist* magazine, which two years later had produced the apocalyptic, but widely acclaimed *Blueprint for Survival*, republished as a book. *Blueprint*, largely written by Teddy Goldsmith, was deeply pessimistic about the future of Western industrial society unless man could be persuaded to return to smaller communities. Not long afterwards he had himself left his bachelor life in London and Paris and settled in three farms near Wadebridge in Cornwall with a group of his friends to begin to practise what he preached.

Teddy Goldsmith was not the only one of Jimmy Goldsmith's circle to be convinced by this bleak diagnosis of the future. John Aspinall shared the same views. He had launched the *Blueprint for Survival* announcing as he did so, 'Gambler that I have always been, brave man that I am, I tremble before the oncoming storm.' In February 1974 Aspinall even helped his old friend Teddy Goldsmith's campaign as an Ecology Party candidate in the General Election that Edward Heath called in February in the wake of the miners' strike. Teddy had decided to stand in his father's old constituency, the Eye division of Suffolk, and Aspinall provided a camel to catch the eye of the press. Aspinall and the Marquis of Londonderry have remained supporters of the *Ecologist* magazine ever since.

In the years since they had left Oxford Teddy Goldsmith and John Aspinall had travelled together looking for rare and wild animals, some of which were later to be found at Aspinall's private zoo in the fifty-five-acre grounds of his home, Howlett's near Canterbury in Kent. The two men had remained very close. Teddy Goldsmith lost his deposit in the General Election but his brother was not put off. The politics which his friends at the Clermont had advocated had their effect. He realized that they might be right when they urged him to speak up in the public debate, and he had come to the conclusion that the chairman of a public company in Britain and France needed to have a vision of his political future.

Not that he envisaged giving up the pleasures of running his companies, shuffling their assets about according to his own rules as rapidly as he had always done, but he had come to accept his dislike of the establishment. As he told a group of Eton sixth-formers in February, 'For a career in the City one needs to be honourable and trustworthy, but for a career in industry one needs a more determined will to win.' The remark was greeted with more than one knowing smile in the City of London.

By the end of February 1974, when Edward Heath lost his majority in the House of Commons and Harold Wilson returned to Downing Street with a Labour Government with the narrowest of majorities, Goldsmith was still busily tidying up his group's affairs. Three months later he completed the purchase of the Spanish Sanders company, and then in June entered an agreement with Banco Urquijo in Madrid, to extend the food group's activities throughout Spain. At the same time he bought over 400,000 shares in his own Générale Alimentaire from the Rothschild family's Compagnie du Nord, thereby putting GA's ownership and control beyond doubt.

But this was not the furious expansion of two years before. He was aware that there was a time for everything and this was the time to stay out of the limelight. So he was a little surprised when he heard in June 1974 that Jim Slater's former partner, Peter Walker, had organized a dinner at his Westminster home so that the leader of the opposition, Edward Heath, could meet one or two leading businessmen. There were, he was told, to be three principal guests apart from Mr Heath himself, Jim Slater (Peter Walker's former partner in Slater Walker) and two of Jim Slater's other friends, Selim Zilkha and Jimmy Goldsmith. The conversation was to be about how to help the Conservative Party win the election that Harold Wilson would clearly be forced to call before the year was out.

Heath had known Jim Slater for some considerable time. They had met when Heath was leader of the Opposition, living in chambers in Albany off Piccadilly. Jim Slater had advised the future Prime Minister on his personal affairs, and while his own brokers administered the detail of his investments, Slater Walker recommended them. After Heath became Prime Minister, Slater continued to see him from time to time.

Edward Heath liked Jimmy Goldsmith. Perhaps the Tory leader recognized in him something of his own impatience with other people's slowness. Perhaps he saw they shared a distrust of the sometimes ponderous foibles of the democratic process, a suspicion of the English establishment which neither felt quite accepted them, a conviction that they alone might be able to save the nation from the peril that confronted it. Undoubtedly the dinner cemented a political friendship that was to last for a year or more, and it convinced Goldsmith that there could be a political future for him in England if he took care to nurture it.

In the words of one of Mr Heath's friends, 'Ted Heath

saw Jimmy Goldsmith as an example of the new capitalism he admired. For a time he became one of his new heroes like Arnold Weinstock and Jim Slater, the sort of man he could call on to help with money for particular projects, for research help when he needed it, and who could be relied upon to be as annoyed as he was by the failings of the Tory Party organization.' After Peter Walker's dinner Edward Heath asked his new friend to help him win the coming election.

For his part, Goldsmith may have seen qualities in Edward Heath he recognized in himself, just as he saw that politics might be an interesting career, but he was not all that impressed by the ways of politicians. After a meeting with Heath and Willie Whitelaw he was to recall later, 'It was my first real contact with politics, and I couldn't believe the weakness of it all.'

Whitelaw and Heath were a little bewildered by the aggression of his conclusions – Jimmy Goldsmith told them that their advertising was terrible and that they had to reform their constituency organization if they wanted to win the election – and, uncertain how to make the best use of him, they allowed their discussions to tail off for a time during the summer. But in August 1974, with the prospect of a General Election looming, Edward Heath sent another message to Jimmy Goldsmith who was holidaying in a villa in Amalfi rented from Carlo Ponti. Flattered, and curious to know what it would be like to be at the heart of affairs of state, Goldsmith flew back from his holiday early to see Heath and talk about how he could help. He would provide advice, look at ways of raising money – he decided to give a dinner for major industrialists at which they would be asked to support the Tory cause – and provide what other help he could.

Some years earlier, Jimmy Goldsmith had also helped Edward Heath after Jeffrey Archer, then still a young ambitious MP, had approached him to ask for a donation of £100,000 to promote the European cause, and he had agreed. That donation, like every other political donation he was to make, came from his own pocket, not from the Cavenham group. The company made no political donations in 1973, 1974 or 1975. The chairman could do what he liked with his own money; by now he was extremely rich.

But the experience finally left him with the suspicion that the leadership of the Conservative Party were not determined enough to win. When Denis Healey, Labour Chancellor of the Exchequer, had claimed during the campaign that inflation was going down, he had provided detailed research to contradict him. Yet it had not been properly used. He had been left to predict that food prices would soar upwards himself, when he felt the issue could have had a dramatic effect on the election result. The whole experience somewhat depressed him.

Perhaps for some time afterwards Goldsmith harboured the dream of a political career, based on a peerage that a grateful Prime Minister would give him after a Conservative Party victory in October 1974, which would bring in its wake a ministerial appointment to allow him to put his theories into practice. Certainly he believed for a while that Heath would be returned to power by the end of 1975; he even had a bet with 'Tiny' Rowland to that effect; but the dream faded rapidly. For unlike his financial career, he never managed to ensure that his hopes and aspirations in politics coincided with the opportunities. He never managed to hit a winning streak, and no matter how determined he was in the effort to find one, it would always elude him.

Although it was never put to the test there were those commentators who maintained later that the suggestion in Edward Heath's election manifesto for the October Election in 1974 that the Government should draw in outside talents where it could was a direct reference to his desire to see Goldsmith brought into the Government, but for once the financier with the considerable track record for predicting business success could not influence events himself. Edward Heath lost the General Election as Goldsmith had feared privately he might. To cheer himself he took a party of his friends, including Annabel, on holiday to the sun the following day.

After the election Edward Heath offered him political compensation if there was anything he wanted to do, and for his part Jimmy Goldsmith asked if he could reorganize party headquarters, Central Office. If he did so, he told Heath, there was no reason why the Tory Party need lose again. The left, he pointed out forcefully, had already seen the value of having well disciplined local organizations. But the offer was never taken up, and within a matter of months Heath himself was out of power, deposed as leader of the Conservative Party by Margaret Thatcher.

Mrs Thatcher maintained a connection with the Party's rich supporter. She complemented him on the Lubbock lecture he gave at Oxford in December 1974, and thanked him for his support in underwriting the Centre for Policy Studies which Sir Keith Joseph was getting off the ground. But there was no immediate prospect of his political advancement.

He maintained later that within a year he had decided not to waste time on the prospect. 'I don't spend time on futile thought,' he was to say. Certainly by 1977 any of the Tory constituency parties that approached him about the possibility of his becoming their candidate, including the one near his English home in Richmond, were told firmly that he would do them no good – he would bring them too much adverse publicity. It was the reaction of a man who believed he was persecuted unfairly, but who also felt that the persecution placed him apart from the commonplace. It was a notoriety he came to enjoy.

But at the end of 1974 he was still wanting a voice in the public debate, even if he was suspicious of politicians, and that necessitated making speeches. Unlikely as it sounded from a man brought up in the hotels of Europe in December he told the University of Oxford, 'We are ill adjusted to face the great new challenges that confront us. We have been fortunate in that we have been prosperous for a long time. But prolonged prosperity is not good training. People begin to forget why we have this wonderful thing and what produced it. They start believing that it is their god-given right or natural right. They forget fundamental facts ... As a result we draw farther and farther away from reality.'

Yet his apparent suspicion of democracy was also clear, for he went on to argue, 'it was once said that democracy can survive only for so long as the majority is willing to sacrifice the short term for the long term. When this is no longer the case, when the majority is more interested in the short term, then the whole nation becomes a vast rotten borough. It chooses its leaders by the number of short-term inducements that are promised ... To pander to this irresponsibility is evil. The government should make clear our changed circumstances and should explain the perils we face. It must preach civil duties not civil rights.'

He concluded by making a series of suggestions about what a new British government might do. In particular he advocated the consideration of limiting immigration into Britain – 'I believe we should have a plan and that we should have the courage to publish it and explain it even if it does slaughter a few sacred cows.' He also urged the development of British agriculture and British industry. 'Industry should be allowed to produce its accounts to reflect the real results of its activities,' and he went on, 'We should re-define the word "profits" to mean only the surplus available for distribution to shareholders after having allowed for that amount of investment necessary for a reasonable rate of growth.' They were the opinions of many a Tory businessman, but Goldsmith concluded in rather more sweeping style with an analysis of what would happen if Britain did not pay attention to his, and others', conclusions.

'If we continue to avoid facing the facts then very soon we will be heading for disaster. The disaster will probably occur as a result of a run on sterling. This could be the result of the demise of the Social Contract and runaway inflation, or of a new war in the Middle East, or of a new upsurge in the costs of raw materials, or of the withdrawal or hot Arab funds on deposit with us, or for one or a combination of other reasons.'

He added darkly, 'If it does occur then we will be on the merry-go-round to hell.' Indeed, he concluded, 'There is no limit to the rate of inflation that could ensue and we would be heading speedily to hyper-inflation on a Weimar scale. Of course we would get a little temporary respite on the way. We would get a national government. We would obtain a major international loan on the security of our foreign investments. But it would only be temporary. We would lose what was left of our international credit and we would then have difficulties in buying the raw materials to keep our industry operating and in paying for the food to feed our population. That is when our present system would collapse. Chaos would ensue and out of the disorder would emerge a new kind of order.'

It was a typically Napoleonic exaggeration, and represented a style which was to convince some of his closest friends that his contemplation of a political career in England would always turn out to be fruitless. Yet it was not altogether different from other industrialists' views. It was the grand sweep of the conclusion that made it seem extravagant. His dislike of compromise, particularly when it came to hyperbole, and his inability to control his outbursts against those he saw as his enemies made it impossible. As one friend was to remark later, 'He is simply too intemperate to be a politician. He will say wild things, and he pays no attention to how they will be received. If he could have been rather more temperate then he might have been an important public figure, but he couldn't be, and so he won't.'

As 1974 drew to a close, however, it was a domestic event that had a greater impact on Jimmy Goldsmith's life than thoughts of politics. The disappearance of his old gambling acquaintance, the 7th Earl of Lucan, who had been on holiday with him in Acapulco the previous year, was to do more to destroy what political ambitions he may still have had than any tendency to exaggerate. John Lucan, as he was known, who had inherited nearly a quarter of a million pounds on his father's death in 1963 but had since gambled the bulk of it away on the Clermont's tables, had disappeared after the murder of his children's nanny, Sandra Rivett.

At the time of the murder Goldsmith was in Ireland on business, and on the following day, 8 November 1974, he was still there. He did not attend a lunch given by Lucan's closer friend John Aspinall at his house that day to discuss what might have happened to him. But the assumption that he had been there, and that he knew more about the

Earl's disappearance than he was prepared to say, was to become of considerable significance in his life. It was to make him, for better or worse, a man whose reputation went far beyond a food company.

As Christmas approached, however, 'Lucky' Lucan was a long way from his mind. He was thinking instead about Cavenham's progress. In April Madame Beaux had joined the board of directors, and everything seemed to be progressing remarkably well, particularly in America, as he had predicted it would. He even owned a successful racehorse, Garnishee, which had won the prestigious Massey Ferguson Gold Cup at Cheltenham in December. Sadly he had not been there to see it, and neither had he backed it.

9. The Bank's Choice

Jimmy Goldsmith was a good deal more agitated about the birth of his fifth child than he cared to admit. Certainly the experience of Lady Annabel Birley bearing their child was hardly new, after all their daughter Jemima had been born only a year before, but he was very anxious that this, the second of his English children, should be a boy. So as he paced up and down restlessly waiting for news, he reflected that although neither he nor Annabel had planned on having another child so quickly the accident of her pregnancy might have brought him a prize to treasure, a son to sustain the dynasty he had helped to create again: the Goldsmiths. Granted he already had a French son, Manes, who was nearly sixteen, and for whom he had a deep personal affection, but the boy did not seem to have quite the concentration or determination to perpetuate the family name that his father had shown. Perhaps another son might be more interested in the prospect of ensuring that the family's revived reputation would continue to prosper. So when the news finally came on 30 January 1975 that Lady Annabel Birley had given birth to a healthy baby boy, he was delighted. The next generation of English Goldsmiths had properly begun; perhaps he should talk to Annabel about whether they should get married. A son was a significant event.

One reason why dynasties were on Jimmy Goldsmith's mind as Zacharias was born was that he was on the brink of being officially welcomed into the greatest Jewish banking dynasty in Europe, the one administered under the sign of the red shield by his cousins the Rothschilds for the past 200 years. Once he had sold his 70 per cent holding in the Paris Discount Bank to the Rothschilds he would find himself with a 7 per cent stake in their family Bank in France, and he knew that would in turn lead to a seat on the board of one of the most celebrated banks in the world. His directorship would represent recognition of his achievements over the past ten years, and signal to everyone that the Goldsmith family fortunes had been firmly and permanently revived. Never again would anyone be able to suggest, as some newspapers in England had done, that his success was based on little more than adept financial conjuring, the tricks of a prestidigitator who worked with a balance sheet and shares rather than wearing an upturned top hat. No one could impugn the methods or the traditions of a member of the Rothschild bank. The Rothschilds symbolized respectability and substance, and there could be no doubt of that. They had, after all, not only financed Bismarck's Germany, but also organized the £4 million loan that enabled Disraeli to make Britain the principal stockholder in the Suez Canal. The fact that the deal would also raise him some £4½ million, a great deal more than his godfather Baron James de Rothschild had left him in his will, was beside the point.

In the meantime, however, there were also Cavenham's affairs to be dealt with. For as Goldsmith concluded his agreement with the Rothschilds, he also settled the deal he had been negotiating in Ireland the previous November – the sale of all the Allied Suppliers shops there for more than £2 million. At the same time he had been preparing to increase Cavenham's holdings in their American supermarket chain, Grand Union. They already had control of the company, but he had plans to buy another 30 per cent of it. Since Cavenham had taken over in the United States his management team, led by Jim Wood, had closed forty-seven small shops and opened nineteen new ones. They had also stopped giving trading stamps to their customers, giving them lower prices instead. The world recession was clearly going to have its effect, but he had seen the signs that America would recover more quickly than Britain. Besides, America was where he believed the long-term future of his businesses was certain to lie.

In England, however, Cavenham was still in a reasonably healthy state. By March 1975 it had earned a profit after tax of £17 million, and had a cash reserve of nearly £30 million. As he put it in his chairman's statement, 'We will pursue our long established policy of concentrating our efforts on our main activities, finding the new capital necessary to support them by eliminating all operations that are either marginal or unrelated to the main stream of our business.' It had been a policy which had worked for him admirably in the preceding years.

But not all his friends in England were able to take such a confident view of the future. One of them, Jim Slater, was beginning to realize that his vast financial and banking empire, which boasted assets of nearly £300 million in 1972, was in danger of crumbling. Nor did Goldsmith quite realize what effect that would have on him.

Two years before, in 1973, the British stock market had fallen by 30 per cent, and in 1974 by a further 50 per cent, until it was lower than it had been after Dunkirk and a German invasion seemed imminent. The economic future for everyone, especially Jim Slater, looked bleak. In the first three months of 1975, however, the *Financial Times* 30 share index doubled, and up with it went Slater Walker's shares, trebling in the process. But, as Jim Slater later recalled, 'In its fight for survival Slater Walker had to a large extent lost its *raison d'être* and no longer had a worthwhile role to play. If we survived we would have to find a new identity, and it would take years to build. The failure of so many secondary banks and finance companies, such as Jessel Securities, First National, Triumph and Vavasseur would make investors and the City community continue to worry about a company such as Slater Walker for years to come. I had lost my early enthusiasm, and felt it would be much better for shareholders and for employees if a different solution could be found.'

One person with whom he had discussed his unease was his old backgammon opponent Jimmy Goldsmith, who had, in any case, built up a substantial shareholding in Slater Walker for Cavenham during the previous twelve months. Indeed by the beginning of January 1975 his stake was almost 8 per cent of Slater Walker, and Goldsmith was as anxious as anyone to ensure its future. Inevitably the two men began to talk about the possibility of a merger of their two companies and Goldsmith even discussed it with members of his Générale Occidentale board of directors in France. Jim Slater said later, 'We had several general discussions about the possibility of his master company,

119

Générale Occidentale, acquiring Slater Walker, and we also discussed the idea of Générale Occidentale and Slater Walker equity accounting each other.' But in the end their discussions came to nothing: the details of the merger could never quite be agreed by either side.

In just the same way, not long afterwards Jim Slater's discussions with 'Tiny' Rowland of Lonrho petered out in the wake of a series of bitter accusations about Slater Walker's dealings in the Far East. By May 1975, when Jim Slater told a depressed annual general meeting of the previously high flying company that profits would be at a very low level, he knew he had to cheer himself up. He decided to take four of his friends to the Tulchan estate in Scotland for a little fishing, even though at least one of them – Jimmy Goldsmith – had never fished before in his life. Indeed the sport turned out to be much too slow for Goldsmith's taste, and he decided to try and divert his companions, who included Selim Zilkha and Angus Ogilvy, by offering them substantial bets on who would be the first to land a fish and how much it would weigh. That way at least he could still feel the adrenalin running through his veins as he felt the water creep up his waders. His host was exasperated but amused.

Back in France after the trip, Goldsmith decided to keep on selling those parts of his group that did not fit any longer into the main stream. Within a month he had sold two of his longest established companies, including the Laboratories Grémy-Longuet, which still produced the slimming aid which had sustained him when things had been really difficult. The whole company went to the American Smithkline corporation.

At the same time he was negotiating to go into partnership with the French state-owned Mining and Chemical Corporation for the production and sale of animal foods in France and Belgium. The state corporation would, if the deal came off, become equal partners in his Sanders company. Few people in France realized it, but he was already putting into effect his own Acapulco plan. The withdrawal to America was going ahead, but very quietly. As the year progressed, however, it was to speed up.

In July the Sanders deal was completed, and in August

he sold off what had once been another staple of Cavenham's development, the slimming breads Slimcea and Procea. They were sold, together with the baking interests and the trademarks, to one of their two principal remaining customers, Spillers. Dietary foods and slimming aids were no longer part of Jimmy Goldsmith's plans.

In the meantime Jim Slater had introduced Jimmy Goldsmith to another of his friends, David Frost, the television presenter. He and Jim Slater had become close friends over the previous three years, since Jim Slater had found Frost a suitable quoted company – Equity Enterprises – for him to use as a basis for his business interests. Indeed Slater Walker and David Frost had both purchased significant stakes in it. In January 1973 Slater Walker organized Frost's bid to take over Hemdale.

Just as Slater and Peter Walker had been the means of Goldsmith's introduction to political power, and his friendship with Edward Heath, so another of Slater's friends, David Frost, was to be his introduction to a second political relationship, this time with the Labour Prime Minister Harold Wilson. It was another example of his circle of affluent friends being widened, but into a world that he did not entirely understand: the man raised in a world of hotel suites and closeted comforts where no one questioned their right to caviar and champagne, was certainly not familiar with the hustings of politics, particularly in the Labour Party. His was also a world away from most journalists, another group he hardly understood. To someone who had barely contemplated the thought that life could be anything other than comfortable, even luxurious by some standards, the notion that this might lead to disapproval or even envy among some came as a shock. As 1975 went on it became clear to him that not everyone shared either his lifestyle or his opinions.

Indeed there were already signs that the tide of praise for the 1960s and 1970s 'whizz kids' was beginning to turn. In May 1975 the *Economist* published a lighthearted but sceptical article about the value of Goldsmith and Slater to investors, concluding that both men's performances looked a little tired.

The brief piece in the influential magazine's investment pages made Goldsmith distinctly angry. It was as if everything he had battled to achieve was only fit to be belittled in an aside, and he saw it as further evidence of the conspiracy he was sure had been built up against him in the British press. It was a feeling he had nurtured since his experiences with the *Sunday Times* in 1971, when he had complained to Roy Thomson, then the paper's proprietor, about the behaviour of one of his reporters on the paper's Business News. Then he had wondered if it was not just the work of one of his commercial rivals, putting ideas into the heads of journalists who wrote about him, but as time had passed he had become more and more convinced that there was some sort of conspiracy to discredit him and belittle his achievements. Certainly he trusted one or two English journalists: the *Sunday Telegraph*'s City Editor, Patrick Hutber, the *Daily Mail*'s City Editor, Patrick Sergeant, and one or two others. He was even prepared to accept that most journalists were honest and hardworking, though he suspected they were also a little too gullible. But he was certain that some were working for purposes other than those they pretended to be pursuing. It was a thought that would come to preoccupy him increasingly in the months ahead. He was determined not to be intimidated by the conspiracy.

Less than a month later his worst suspicions were confirmed, again by the *Sunday Times*, but this time by its colour magazine. There on the cover was Annabel Birley sitting close beside the Earl of Lucan, while inside was a series of pictures of Lucan with Goldsmith and his other friends on his fortieth birthday holiday in Acapulco in 1973. 'It was the cover which annoyed me the most. It consisted of a photograph taken after lunch during the Acapulco holiday as a sort of joke,' he says today. 'But printed on its own it seemed to suggest that Annabel was somehow romantically linked with Lucan which of course was a perfect nonsense.' There was also a painting inside by Dominic Elwes, who had also been with them in Acapulco, of him at a Clermont luncheon table together with Lord Lucan, the stockbroker Stephen Raphael, Charles Benson of the *Daily Express*, the Earl of Suffolk,

John Aspinall and Peter West. The painting and the photographs were accompanied by an article by James Fox who suggested that he had attended the lunch John Aspinall gave the day after Lucan's disappearance.

Goldsmith was furious. Annabel hardly knew Lucan, and the newspaper seemed to be implying that he was somehow involved with Lord Lucan's disappearance. Someone had betrayed him by selling the photographs. He wanted to know who. But he felt the article was typical of his treatment by the English press.

He would fight back as hard as he could, and he would make sure that Dominic Elwes understood how upset he was by this betrayal of friendship. 'A friend of mine saw him while he was painting and said that I would find it objectionable but he answered that he did not care. It was Elwes who organized the article and introduced Fox to all those concerned,' he was to say later. 'My only reaction *vis à vis* Elwes was that I said I would never see him again.'

In fact, apart from the reference to the lunch, the Acapulco photograph, and the painting of the Clermont table, there was no other mention of him in the piece; and although his first inclination had been to issue a libel writ, he allowed himself to be persuaded not to do so. Instead he asked for and accepted an apology from the editor. There was no point in making an unnecessary fuss about it, but he was determined not to let the matter rest.

Mark Birley, who was still married to Annabel and still harboured hopes of her returning to him, even though they were now on the brink of divorce, was also very unhappy about the *Sunday Times* magazine article. As the *Daily Mail*'s Nigel Dempster was to report three months later, Mark Birley decided to ban Elwes from both his nightclub Annabel's, and the other Mayfair club that he had started more recently, Mark's. Dempster also reported that Mark Birley's son Robin had written to Elwes saying he had made life intolerable for him at Eton, and the family did not want to see him again.

Elwes, who had suffered from bouts of severe depression in the past, and, to the concern of his friends, had apparently tried to kill himself on a number of occasions, took the ban from the circle that he had spent so much of his life being close to very much to heart. He was especially upset at not being able to talk to his cousin Annabel to whom he felt he had been particularly close, but she seemed just as angry with him. Within a week he had decided to go away to the South of France to think things over.

On the flight to Nice he happened to meet Nigel Dempster, who later reported, 'I drove him to his apartment near where I was staying and we saw each other every day for a week. He spoke often of suicide.' Elwes told him that his father was dying a horrible death, his mother was terribly ill, that a relation had invested all his money very badly, and he went on, 'My old friends have turned on me because of the Lucan business. I have been accused of selling photographs of Annabel and Lucky Lucan to the newspapers ... Can't people understand that I've never taken a photograph, never even had a camera ... Mark, whom I've known for forty years, has now banned me from the clubs and he says he never wants to see me again. Annabel has said the same and their son Robin has written me this wretched letter.'

Elwes told Nigel Dempster that he had also lost Goldsmith's friendship. 'I can't understand why they are all doing this to me. I have always been a good friend to them, and when Annabel and Jimmy were going through a bad time it was me who helped her get over it.'

By the first week in September Dominic Elwes, the forty-four-year-old son of Royal portrait painter Simon Elwes, father of three children by his wife, the heiress Tessa Kennedy, with whom he had eloped in 1958, was dead. He had killed himself by taking an overdose of drugs, leaving two suicide notes. The shorter, it was later reported, read, 'I curse Mark and Jimmy from beyond the grave. I hope they are happy now.'

Dominic Elwes's suicide was destined to make Jimmy Goldsmith the subject of wider press reporting than ever before. From now on he would be someone known not only to readers of financial pages but to a much wider public. But before that happened another friend was to drag him into the limelight from the seclusion of his own world of private dinner parties and holidays with his families and friends. By the middle of September a series of bitter accusations and counter accusations about Slater Walker's relationship with the Haw Par company in Singapore had begun to weaken confidence in Jim Slater's group. Indeed by the end of September the British press had started to report stories of corruption in the company's dealings in the Far East, and they continued to do so repeatedly over the next fortnight. By the middle of October Slater Walker shares had fallen in value to under 50 pence. As Jim Slater put it later, 'For the first time I began to realize that I should consider resigning from the Slater Walker board.'

Within a few days Slater had discussed the prospect of his resignation with Gordon Richardson, the Governor of the Bank of England, for, as he recalled later, 'I could see that if I resigned the growing unpleasantness of the Spydar situation would be removed from the company, and that it would clear the way for an independent board to negotiate a settlement with Singapore. I knew there would be no hope of the Singapore authorities ever agreeing a settlement with me at the helm.'

After discussing it again, Richardson and Slater came to the conclusion that the obvious man to replace him as chairman of the vast company, which in March 1972 had gross assets of nearly £300 million, was Jimmy Goldsmith. He had a substantial shareholding in the company and Slater trusted him. On Wednesday 16 October 1975 when they were having one of their regular dinners together, Jim Slater put the idea to him. Goldsmith urged his friend to think it over carefully at the weekend before he made his mind up, but they did discuss what sort of board might be acceptable to take over as well as what sort of financial backing might be available from the Bank of England to support the now very shaky Slater Walker. By Monday morning Jim Slater had made up his mind to resign and telephoned Goldsmith to tell him.

In the next few days Slater held further discussion with the Governor of the Bank of England, and so did Goldsmith. The new chairman of Slater Walker wanted to bring into the company with him a number of new directors to re-establish confidence; and he wanted an assurance that the government would provide the necessary funds to see the company through its difficulties. By Thursday the details had been agreed. Jimmy Goldsmith would become chairman and temporary chief executive of Slater Walker and the new directors had been settled. They would include Lord Rothschild, and Ivor Kennington of N. M. Rothschild's bank, Charles Hambro and Peter Hill-Wood of Cavenham's own merchant bankers, Hambros, and Sir Ronald Leach, the noted City accountant, would become consultant. In the meantime Jimmy Goldsmith had also told Madame Beaux she would be spending a good deal of her time in the months ahead working on the future of Slater Walker rather than GO or Cavenham.

Jimmy Goldsmith's decision to take over had not been entirely altruistic. He and Anglo-Continental had built up a considerable shareholding in the company, and he wanted it suitably protected. He was also anxious to help a friend, and to see that the most successful of the secondary banks in Britain did not founder, taking with it the savings of large numbers of ordinary investors, most of whom could not afford to lose them. It was to make him a very public figure indeed.

As the *Investors' Chronicle* noted the following week, 'Only the abdication of the Queen, one supposes, would command more column inches.' Indeed, interest in the press in Slater Walker's affairs became almost overwhelming. The *Daily Telegraph* captured the mood of the entire British press when it reported, 'Last night's changes at the top of Slater Walker Securities marked the end of one of the most remarkable stories in the City's long history – the rise of builder's son Mr Jim Slater – and his creation of possibly the most remarkable investment machine ever seen.'

'One of Jimmy Goldsmith's first priorities, when he returns from Paris on Tuesday to pick up the reins, will be to sort out the $29 million-worth of loans made by Slater Walker Securities to Haw Par, the Singapore group which it had controversially acquired in 1972,' the *Sunday Times* reported. In a profile the paper concluded that Goldsmith had now emerged as 'the last survivor of the new financial phoenixes whose stars shone so brightly and dramatically in the 1960s and early 1970s. But although in some ways his early business career showed parallels with Jim Slater, Malcolm Horsman and John Bentley and the millionaire-a-minute property men, he is a very different kind of animal.' But the paper refrained from describing exactly what kind of animal he was.

Few of the press reports in England, for example, pointed out exactly how much he knew about Slater Walker, or even that there had been discussions about a merger earlier in the year, but every report had acknowledged that in France his Générale Occidentale had become an intensely respectable company. Its board now contained representatives of Credit Lyonnais, Compagnie d'Electricitie, Lazard Frères, Rothschilds and the Union des Assurances de Paris (France's largest insurance company). The Caisse des Depots (France's national savings bank) and Renault also had significant shareholdings in the company. Comparatively few, however, either noticed or made the connection that one of the new directors of Slater Walker was Monsieur Dominique Leca of the Union des Assurances in Paris.

While some of the other financial whizz-kids of the early 1970s had relied principally on a blind confidence that their own abilities would carry them through any economic difficulties that might arise, Goldsmith had set about constructing a stable and respectable French holding company which would be able to survive the economic disasters he had seen coming. The man who had begun as fiercely independent financial operator, who had not been anxious to lose his freedom of action by accepting the more cautious attitudes of a board of directors, had quietly changed. He could still decide, but others now deserved to be taken into account.

Not that he had suddenly come to believe that he should fill the boards of any of his companies with an assorted group of aristocrats with little interest in or experience of business. He had not been sucked into that view of the establishment. He was still a rebel to that tradition. Indeed he had told a conference of editors and publishers only a fortnight before taking over at Slater Walker, 'Britain must be a meritocracy. The best, no matter what their background, must reach the top. Excellence must unreservedly be encouraged. Our present educational system is incompatible with, indeed hostile to, this obvious objective. Our private sector, dominated by the public schools, consists, with trivial exceptions, of students selected on the criteria of wealth and birth. It is absurd to believe that this nation can for long tolerate such a system of selection.' The remarks brought a congratulatory leader from the *Daily Mirror*.

In what was almost a defence of his own actions over the years he also claimed in the same speech, 'If you are an industrial nation overpopulated, competing for world trade to pay for the imports of food to feed your people, then you need a few winners whether you like them or not.' In the midst of his speech's political analysis, which included an attack on left-wing infiltration of the Labour Party, the undemocratic nature of trade union elections, and the need for reform of the Conservative Party, Goldsmith had not completely forgotten that too many people in Britain seemed determined to deny him the credit for his achievements which he thought he had earned.

Hardly had he been chairman of Slater Walker for a month, however, when Dominic Elwes entered his life again. A requiem service for the painter was held at the Jesuit Church in Farm Street, Mayfair. Jimmy Goldsmith did not go to the memorial service: 'In the previous ten years I might have seen Elwes twenty times at the most. He was a friend and cousin of Annabel but only a very old acquaintance of mine.' Addresses had been given by both John Aspinall and Kenneth Tynan. After the service one of Elwes's cousins, Tremayne Rodd, had punched Aspinall in the face. Although Aspinall had tried to laugh it off with the comment 'I'm used to dealing with wild animals' it had nevertheless caught the attention of the man who was to become Goldsmith's most public enemy, Richard Ingrams, the editor of the satirical magazine *Private Eye*. As Ingrams was to recall in *Goldenballs*, his book about the subsequent events, it was only when the Farm Street incident took place that he thought: 'Something is going on here that

Above: *(left)* Digby Neave (*Keystone*); *(right)* Selim Zilkha (*London Express*)

Left: John Aspinall having been punched by Tremayne Rodd, the late Dominic Elwes's cousin. The incident provoked *Private Eye*'s coverage of the events surrounding Elwes's death and led to Goldsmith's criminal libel case (*Keystone*)

Dominic Elwes, Lady Annabel Goldsmith's cousin, who committed suicide in 1975 (*Syndication International*)

The 7th Earl of Lucan, whose distant friendship with Goldsmith also stimulated *Private Eye* (*London Express*)

Sir James Goldsmith and Lady Annabel Birley arriving at Bow Street Magistrates Court in July 1976 for the hearing of his criminal libel prosecution against *Private Eye* (*Central Press*)

Lady Annabel Goldsmith in 1981 with four of her six children: Jane Birley (now Mrs Jane Colchester), Jemima (aged seven), Zacharias (aged six) and baby Benjamin (*Daily Express*)

Sir James and Lady Annabel in Italy in 1979

Sir James Goldsmith with the first dummy edition of his British news magazine (*Syndication International*)

may make an interesting article for *Private Eye*. What it was or who precisely were the parties involved, I had at that time no clear idea.'

So while Goldsmith devoted himself to getting under way the investigation of Slater Walker which he had asked Rothschilds and Hambros to carry out, Ingrams began to look into the events at Farm Street. The first person he contacted was Dominic Elwes's friend and companion for a week in the South of France that summer, Nigel Dempster, the *Daily Mail*'s gossip columnist, whom Ingrams had often relied on for his 'encyclopaedic knowledge of high society'.

After their conversation Dempster sat down and wrote an eight-page memorandum on Elwes and his friends at the Clermont Club and elsewhere, which he then posted to Ingrams. 'It contained as much as I knew at the time,' he said later, 'but it did not say Jimmy had been at the lunch at Aspinall's the day after Lucan disappeared.' In fact Dempster and Goldsmith had never met, although they had spoken on the telephone. Nevertheless both men were to form a strong impression of each other. For Ingrams, who had also never met Goldsmith, Dempster's memorandum, and Elwes's suicide, became part of his conviction that this rather too rich, rather too flamboyant financier, who seemed to disregard convention, was a subject who demanded much more careful examination in *Private Eye*.

The two men, over the next year and a half, were to become two of the most public enemies Britain had seen in the previous fifty years, warring constantly in courts of law or in statements in the press, yet never speaking, only nodding at each other occasionally across the crowded courtrooms in which their feud was being acted out. Throughout, Goldsmith would be seen smiling in what Ingrams would later call his 'wintry way', while Ingrams looked as faintly puzzled as he usually did, as though trying to keep a straight face. It was also the clash of two styles, Ingrams being the son of a merchant banker, retiring, conservative, corduroy-jacketed, serious-minded (in spite of his apparent appetite for the scurrilous) who had given up drinking and smoking, and who played the organ in his local church near his home in Berkshire where he lived with his wife and children. It was a sharp contrast to how Jimmy Goldsmith appeared to Ingrams. As Ingrams's friend Alan Watkins later pointed out perceptively, it was the clash of the conservative Ingrams with the liberal Goldsmith. But both men shared one important characteristic. They were equally determined.

After reading Dempster's memorandum Ingrams decided that rather than concentrate simply on the events outside the Jesuit Church in Farm Street, *Private Eye* should consider the career of James Goldsmith, because, as he recorded later, 'Goldsmith was more than a rich banker ... he had, with the approval of the Bank of England just taken over the chairmanship of Slater Walker from Jim Slater.' Indeed, Goldsmith came to believe that he had been used as a target by the magazine to discredit the City and the Bank of England. 'If Slater Walker could be converted into a major scandal, in view of its colossal public impact (it was headlines day after day) this would discredit the City. That is why the moderate socialist ministers of that time wanted to contain the problem whereas the far left were trying to do everything to make the bomb explode. If they could discredit me they would discredit by association those who came in with me and the Bank of England.'

In the Christmas edition of *Private Eye*, which came out on 12 December 1975, Ingrams ran a story about Goldsmith and Elwes, which had been written for him by his colleague Patrick Marnham with some help from another of *Private Eye*'s regular contributors, Michael Gillard. Entitled 'All's Well That Ends Elwes', it was to complete the transformation of Jimmy Goldsmith into a public figure and yet it was almost entirely based on the mistaken impression that he had been present at a lunch given by John Aspinall the day after 'Lucky' Lucan had disappeared. It implied that Goldsmith had played the dominant part in obstructing the course of justice and assisting the fugitive Earl.

'When I first heard about the article I was in Singapore,' Goldsmith said later, 'negotiating a settlement to the Haw

Par affair for Slater Walker. My secretary sent the piece to me, and I did not know what to do about it. For a week I thought I wouldn't do anything at all.'

But when he returned to England he went to a lunch given by Paul Johnson, the former editor of the left-wing political weekly the *New Statesman*. 'That night people there urged me to do something. When I asked what they would do, they advised me to throw the book at *Private Eye*.' So when *Private Eye* carried a further article about him on 9 January 1976, this time linking him with the imprisoned T. Dan Smith, who had been convicted of corrupting local councillors in the North East of England, because one of his solicitors and a friend, Eric Levine, had connections with Smith, Goldsmith decided to act.

Three days later he issued sixty-three writs for libel against *Private Eye* and against thirty-seven of its distributors, and, in a step not taken against an editor in an English court for more than thirty years, he also informed the magazine that he intended to apply to the High Court for permission to bring proceedings for criminal libel. He had found a little opened book to throw at them.

Although there had been a steady trickle of criminal libel cases, the most celebrated case against an editor in the twentieth century had been in 1923 when Lord Alfred Douglas had accused Winston Churchill of deliberately losing the Battle of Jutland in order to cash in some shares on the American stock market. Douglas was sentenced to six months. In 1891 Lord Alfred's close friend Oscar Wilde had brought a case against Douglas's father, the Marquis of Queensbury, but he had lost it. Indeed, indirectly it had led to his downfall, and two years' hard labour in Reading Gaol.

Nevertheless, as Goldsmith's friend Digby Neave put it later, 'Jimmy saw himself as a knight in shining armour, riding into battle against people who had been attacking his friends, and himself. Possibly it was misguided. There was no possible gain in it for him, in fact there was everything to lose.'

Bringing an action for criminal libel was a characteristically exaggerated act. It bore all the hallmarks of impetuousness, and, worse, it seemed to display an unpleasant, vengeful streak in his character with its threat of imprisonment for Ingrams if he were convicted. More than any other single act, it was to cost Goldsmith not only public sympathy but also the possibility of a political career in England. Once again it seemed Jimmy Goldsmith did not care how he appeared; this was not true, he did care, but he fundamentally misjudged how most people who did not know him would react. It made him appear a monster.

Perhaps one other event helped to convince him of the rightness of the fight. Three nights before he issued the sixty-three libel writs, he had been a guest at a dinner party given by his friend David Frost. The guests of honour were Harold Wilson (then still Labour Prime Minister) and his wife Mary, although a group of television people were also there as well as Mr Wilson's aide and adviser Marcia Williams, later Lady Falkender. The conversation was about television. Just before Christmas David Frost had sent the Prime Minister a personal packet to Chequers containing Robert Blake's book on Prime Ministers. It contained the germ of an idea for a television series Sir Harold might make after he left office, a Prime Minister on Prime Ministers. The dinner was to anger some of the Prime Minister's friends, when they heard about it afterwards, because they believed he had let it be known he might be intending to resign before telling his Labour Party colleagues.

It was not the first time David Frost had tried to arrange a dinner for Jimmy Goldsmith and Harold Wilson. The previous autumn, before the changes at Slater Walker, he had invited both Slater and Goldsmith to dinner with Sir Harold (as he became after leaving Downing Street) but the Prime Minister had cancelled at the last moment and asked his press secretary Joe Haines to tell Frost he could not come.

As he told Haines, who later recorded the incident in *The Politics of Power*, he could not as head of a Labour Government be seen to be dining privately with City of London financiers, especially as he had made it a theme of his speeches over the years to condemn 'those who make money rather than earn money'. Nevertheless barely a month afterwards David Frost did take Goldsmith to

Downing Street to introduce him to the Prime Minister. The reason for the meeting was to discuss French economic planning techniques, but Sir Harold also indicated while he was there that the task at Slater Walker, which had not been easy when he had taken over, was not likely to be made any easier by opposition from within the City of London. Harold Wilson told him that he would need all the support he could get.

By then, however, Goldsmith had found another supporter in Downing Street, the Prime Minister's able but argumentative adviser Lady Falkender. Certainly there was little love lost between either Sir Harold Wilson or Lady Falkender and *Private Eye*. The magazine had persistently attacked them both, and showed no sign of stopping. Encouraged, Goldsmith decided it was time someone stood up to the magazine and taught it a stern lesson, and that he was in the best position to do it because he had been so clearly maligned. By the time the battle was over Jimmy Goldsmith, Annabel Birley and Lady Falkender were to be close friends.

To take on the battle at all was the gesture of a man who saw himself as being apart from the ordinary, who believed that he was in a position to right an obvious wrong, and who felt he was the only one capable of doing it. But nevertheless it appeared to be the belligerent action of a man restless for a personal and political advancement, the violent action of a tycoon who was determined that his views and no one else's should be heard, and was determined to crush any criticism of him or his friends. He looked like a vindictive Goliath smiting a tiny, almost insignificant David.

Entered into in some haste, but with a decisiveness that had become his principal asset in business, the battle against *Private Eye* led Jimmy Goldsmith into areas he did not understand, against a magazine that he did not know or comprehend – until he found himself fighting a battle that he might be able to win legally but only at the cost of sacrificing any reputation he might have hoped for among a significant section of English society. He would say publicly that it had never mattered to him, but the wounds were to become very deep.

By the time it was over he would be glad he had already decided to conduct more and more business in America, he would have come to the conclusion that the life of a public figure in Britain was impossible: that any achievement was irrelevant. He would have decided to leave the country to its own fate. Any interest he kept in Britain would be largely to amuse him, to provide him with a platform when he needed it.

In the meantime he saw no particular need to conceal his relationship with Lady Annabel Birley. It was no secret in any case, even though he disliked anyone prying into his life, whether about his business or his personal affairs. So when his old friend Sam White, the Paris correspondent of the London *Evening Standard* suggested to him in the Travellers Club in Paris shortly after the New Year that perhaps he should clear up the confusion about his two lives once and for all, he decided to think about it. That weekend he invited White to lunch at his and Ginette's house in the Rue Monsieur and after lunch he drafted a letter which explained his two families. White was to be allowed to show the letter to the *Evening Standard* lawyers who, the Australian-born correspondent pointed out, might otherwise have been rather reluctant to see the paper print such a story about a man who had just issued sixty-three libel writs. Goldsmith just laughed.

White reported finally on 30 January, 'It is a remarkable situation made even more so because there is no attempt at concealment (no 'Tycoon's Secret Love-Nest Uncovered situation here) and again, as far as I know, no question of divorce.' Indeed he also pointed out that Ginette's son Manes was godfather to Zacharias, while Isabel was godmother to Jemima, which served only to confuse further those who tried to maintain that Goldsmith's dual life could only have been possible if it were clandestine.

Sam White ended by wondering if British political life were ready to accept a man in such a curious matrimonial situation, but he did not report – as the received wisdom among British journalists was later to maintain he had done – that Jimmy Goldsmith was considering a career in British politics.

In fact, as he prepared to go on holiday to Barbados with Jim Slater, Selim Zilkha, John Aspinall and some of his other friends, thoughts of a political career were a long way from his mind. He was a businessman, and he had agreed to buy another 1,800,000 shares in Grand Union, giving him 80 per cent of the company, and to transfer all his holdings in the American supermarket chain to a new American company called Cavenham (USA) Inc. He had also agreed to buy 2 million shares in Slater Walker for his own family and had agreed to pay £460,000 for them. It brought his own holding in Slater Walker to 2·7 million shares, and that was without the company holdings. Then, just as he left for Barbados he announced that Générale Occidentale would take over Cavenham. His removal was already under way.

10. Goldenballs

Jimmy Goldsmith had not had lunch at Number 10 Downing Street before. Indeed he had hardly been inside the building even when Edward Heath had been Prime Minister. He certainly did not know Harold Wilson, the present occupant, all that well. They had only met three times before and never in the formal home of the British Government. He was looking forward to it.

There was to be only one other guest, Lord Ryder, the chairman of the National Enterprise Board. They were to discuss the lessons that French economic planning might be able to teach Britain. He hoped there might also be an opportunity to bring the Prime Minister up to date on Slater Walker now it was almost six months since he had taken over as chairman. Harold Wilson had just announced his intention to resign the premiership in the near future, but Jimmy Goldsmith felt sure he would be interested in the City's reaction to him at Slater Walker. After all, Wilson had warned him that it might not be an easy passage.

Besides there were other things on his mind that April morning as the car turned out of Whitehall into Downing Street. Isabel and her husband Arnaud were clearly fed up with each other. Their marriage was on the verge of breaking up after only two years. Perhaps it was something in the family, he thought, perhaps she wanted to make her own life. He did not really know. He had never been able to understand why she had decided to get married so suddenly and so young. Arnaud was nice enough, but why had she done it? She had not been pregnant. Since then there had been one or two admirers, the young Niarchos, and a Greville, the grandson of the Earl of Warwick, but then Isabel would never lack for admirers. She was a beautiful young woman with her mother's eyes, but with a different personality. No one could quite re-capture that. He could still remember that Saturday in May twenty-two years before when Isabel had been born, and Gypsy had died.

Still, the thought of the battle against *Private Eye*, which was just about to begin, cheered him. The case had been scheduled to start on 8 April, but it had been postponed for five days. He did not intend to go to court to hear the case, but he knew the details of the affidavit he had sworn just before he had gone off to Barbados by heart. It precisely expressed his dislike of *Private Eye*, a dislike he had felt certain Harold Wilson shared after their first meeting at David Frost's house the previous July. It should be straightforward enough a matter to stop their endless insinuations about him and his friends, he thought; but that was to turn out to be a catastrophic misjudgment.

Goldsmith's affidavit had ignored the question of Dominic Elwes's death and dealt simply with Lord Lucan's disappearance. It directly rejected the magazine's suggestion he was the 'richest and most powerful member' of a circle of 'gamblers and boneheads with whom Lord Lucan associated', and which had conspired to obstruct the course of the police enquiries into the murder of Sandra Rivett and John Lucan's disappearance.

Indeed his affidavit had even prompted *Private Eye* to offer an apology, and to explain that they had mistakenly believed he was at John Aspinall's lunch on 8 November 1976. But that was not good enough. Goldsmith was determined to show that they had got away with too much for too long.

What Goldsmith did not know as he stepped out into the unseasonably warm April afternoon after lunch was that his host would leave shortly afterwards for his room at the House of Commons, and tell one or two of his advisers, so his press secretary Joe Haines would recall, that his political secretary Lady Falkender would in all probability be offered a directorship in Cavenham. Haines, who was in the room, remembered later that the Prime Minister had used the phrase, 'Paris is well worth a mass,' when he had told them, referring to the remark usually attributed to Henri IV of France at the end of the sixteenth century when referring to an accommodation he had reached with the Pope. Goldsmith later denied the story ferociously as 'evil nonsense', but that did not prevent Haines from repeating it. Indeed, when Haines's book was published Goldsmith even telephoned Lady Falkender. 'I suggested that we show them just how much we despised them and that I offer her and that she accept a directorship of Cavenham. She refused, no doubt because she was wiser than I.'

At that moment, however, his case for criminal libel against *Private Eye* was much more on his mind. He did not mean to attend the hearing, although he would, of course, go to the court if he were granted leave to bring the case. Nevertheless Mr Lewis Hawser QC was to fire the first salvo in his battle on 13 April 1976 before Mr Justice Wien.

In the panelled court room as the case began, Richard Ingrams and solicitor Eric Levine eyed each other uncertainly during the hearing, but they did not speak: instead they both listened as Lewis Hawser QC told Judge Wein that *Private Eye* had submitted his client James Goldsmith to a 'campaign of vilification', which he detailed by reading a long series of extracts from the magazine. In response Michael Kempster for *Private Eye* quoted the former Lord Chief Justice Lord Coleridge, stating, 'If either by reason of the continued reputation or infamous character of the libel, breach of the peace is likely to ensue, then the libeller should be indicted; but, in the absence of any such conditions, the personal squabble between two private individuals ought not to be permitted by sound law to be the subject of a criminal indictment.'

Richard Ingrams felt confident. He still believed the whole case was 'rather absurd', but the feeling left him as Mr Justice Wein started to sum up on the second day of the hearing, by stating that while he regarded himself as a proponent of the freedom of the press, 'That does not mean that the Press, and in particular any magazine, has a licence to publish scandalous or scurrilous matter which is wholly without foundation.'

He concluded, 'Where a person occupies the position that Mr Goldsmith does, it can be a matter of public importance, and it can well become a matter of public importance when there is an association with the Bank of England and where his integrity has been impugned and a criminal offence has been alleged against him ... I have come to the conclusion that the public interest requires the institution of criminal proceedings.'

Ingrams left the court in a state of shock. 'What no one had thought possible had come to pass,' he said later. 'We had all been treating it almost as a joke, and now I was going to be charged with a criminal offence with the possibility of a prison sentence at the end of it.' Despondent, he went home to Berkshire for the Easter weekend, but when he returned to London he resumed the attack and launched a fund for his defence which the magazine was to name the 'Goldenballs Fund' after Michael Gillard's nickname for their opponent.

To Richard Ingrams and some of his colleagues at *Private Eye* Goldsmith appeared as a man 'extremely sensitive to all forms of criticism, liable to fly off the handle at any time', but they also wondered if their reference to Eric Levine in their article on 9 January 1976 might not have meant that they had actually stumbled on 'some potential source of embarrassment or worse' to Goldsmith. In the next three months they resolved to find out everything they could about both men. It was a decision that was to make the battle more uncompromising than ever.

Yet even now Jimmy Goldsmith had still not finally decided to go ahead with the action against Richard Ingrams for criminal libel. In *Private Eye*'s words, he was 'fingering with some trepidation the antique blunderbuss which Mr Justice Wien in a fit of untypical exuberance has put into his hands.' Indeed the battle was not even joined because James Comyn QC, *Private Eye*'s new barrister, was strongly recommending that they reach an out-of-court settlement with him. Comyn had already received an indication from Lewis Hawser of the terms on which a settlement would be acceptable to Goldsmith. These included damages of up to £20,000, apologies to be printed in *Private Eye* and two other newspapers, as well as an agreement that the magazine would not mention either Goldsmith or Levine for five years and thereafter only do so after any material about either had been submitted to them forty-eight hours before publication. The final demand in the settlement that Lewis Hawser suggested to his opposing Q C was that the names of the writers of the offending articles in *Private Eye* be revealed to his client. Goldsmith was most anxious, he indicated to Comyn, to know who his attackers were.

After a frantic weekend of phone calls, however, the negotiations broke down. Although Goldsmith had been prepared to waive his claim for damages and the five years' ban on the magazine mentioning him, he still insisted on the vetting procedure for both himself and Levine and on being provided with the names of the authors. As Goldsmith put it later, 'I did not feel I could let Eric Levine down, and let him suffer alone.'

So on Monday, 10 May, Richard Ingrams himself imposed a deadline for a settlement of his own which included accepting the publication of an apology, *Private Eye* paying the costs of the case and a guarantee to check information in advance. He was not especially dismayed when the deadline he set for 4 o'clock that day passed, because, as he recorded later, 'Thinking about it, the more reluctant I became to do any deal with Goldsmith whatsoever.' He went on, 'I suppose if I am to be honest, another reason was that in spite of all the stress, part of me was enjoying the excitement of the case and did not want it to end at this point.' The feud between the two men had now properly begun. But before it got fully under way, another drama was to overtake the now publicly angry tycoon, and this time it was not one of his own making.

The weekend before the settlement negotiations with *Private Eye* had broken down, the *Sunday Times* had revealed that Harold Wilson's resignation honours list had run into difficulties. The list, drawn up, according to the newspaper, with the help of Lady Falkender, had met with objections from the Political Honours Scrutiny Committee, and the paper also reported that Harold Wilson himself had deleted one or two names from the list, including, it later transpired, the award of a peerage for his friend David Frost. The newspaper also mentioned that difficulties had arisen over the award of a life peerage to 'a City financier'.

Nine days after the negotiations with *Private Eye* had

broken down the *Daily Express* ran as its main front page story – under the headline 'It's Lord Goldsmith' – the revelation that he was to be given a peerage. Within hours a full-scale political row had broken out over his relations with Harold Wilson, and over his reported political ambitions. It was a row which would damage his public image in England almost as much as his battle with *Private Eye*, for the two became confused in many minds; but Jimmy Goldsmith had never asked for, or been offered, a peerage.

He had only been offered a knighthood, and the first he had known about that was when he received a telephone call in Paris from Harold Wilson shortly before the *Daily Express* story appeared. Wilson said, 'You have not replied to my letter.' Goldsmith replied, perplexed, 'What letter?' and was told. 'The one offering you a knighthood.' The formal letter had been sent by mistake to his former home in Chester Terrace, on the edge of Regent's Park, but he was by then living in Tregunter Road, South Kensington.

Although he did not entirely understand why he was being awarded a knighthood – 'I thought it might have something to do with Slater Walker,' he said later – he accepted the offer formally. There was no doubt he felt flattered by the honour, but the explanation later widely reported, that his political ambitions had meant he was seeking a peerage as a route to the House of Lords, was no longer true. That might once have been the case. He was usually a supporter of the Conservative Party, even though he despaired of their policies. To be awarded a knighthood by a Labour Prime Minister, therefore, somewhat surprised him. Joe Haines, who had seen the honours list in Downing Street as it was being compiled, acknowledged later that Jimmy Goldsmith's name had been put forward for a knighthood – and never for anything else – by Lady Falkender. Goldsmith himself has said, 'All I could think was that I had been caught up in an internal row among Harold Wilson's friends and advisers. I knew Lady Falkender, just as I knew Lord Goodman, who had been acting as my legal adviser, particularly over Slater Walker's dealings in Singapore.' He later became convinced, as

Richard Ingrams also reported, that the story in the *Daily Express* had somehow been leaked. Some friends later attributed the row to Goldsmith's failure to marry Annabel Birley, whose brother-in-law, Sir Max Rayne, was a friend of Goodman and had been elevated to a peerage in the same honours list.

After the honours list was finally published on 27 May, the late George Hutchinson commented in *The Times*, 'Sir Harold Wilson's retirement from office, to all appearances well managed at first and dignified by his own appointment as a Knight of the Garter, has been irretrievably damaged. No honours list, resignation or otherwise, has ever been attended by such farce ... no individual recipient, however deserving, can feel altogether happy. Who could wish for inclusion in a roll call giving rise to universal astonishment and derision?' Hutchinson pointed out that Goldsmith was a 'declared contributor to Tory Party funds.'

The damage had been done. Although he would later receive the Legion d'Honneur in France from President Giscard d'Estaing without attracting anything like the publicity, he was tarred in many minds as a man too anxious for his own advancement. The announcement of an enquiry into who leaked the names recommended for honours did nothing to settle the affair down. Indeed Sir Philip Allen, a former permanent secretary to the Home Office, after interviewing civil servants but none of the Prime Minister's political office, failed to discover who was responsible. Nevertheless forever afterwards members of the Labour Party would regale each other with stories about Goldsmith's knighthood. Together with the *Private Eye* prosecution, and the suspicion in the City of London that he had always been more interested in shuffling companies than in anything else, his knighthood, whether it had been a peerage or not, contrived to make him one of the most controversial public figures to emerge in Britain since the war.

As Michael Davie reported in the *Observer* before May was out, 'The time has come, it appears, when we must begin to puzzle over the phenomenon of Mr James M. Goldsmith, the chairman of the Cavenham Food Group ...

Last week he turned up in the news in three ways. He was the victim of a lead story in the *Daily Express* headlined 'It's Lord Goldsmith' – victim because the universal gasp of amazement must have pained him. He went before a High Court judge to seek another libel action against the magazine *Private Eye* . . . and he attended a special meeting of shareholders to ask them to approve his proposals for extending Cavenham's interests in France through an arcane shuffling of shares back and forth across the Channel.'

Expressing the surprise of many who had been only dimly aware of him, Davies continued, 'Until recently, Goldsmith was simply a playboy, or ex-playboy, who had built up a food company at high speed. Lately, though, his friends have noted a new seriousness about him, and he has started taking an interest in politics. What is more, politicians have been taking an interest in him. When big business men show signs of going political, it behoves the rest of us to pay attention.'

Ironically, Davies's conclusion would have been more accurately written two years before. By the time it appeared, the weekend before Sir Harold Wilson's resignation honours list was finally announced, the ambivalence that Goldsmith had always felt about England and its politics was resolving itself into a despair for the country. There had been moments two years before when he still believed there could be some kind of political future for him in Britain but they had quietly disappeared. There were things about the country and about its political leadership, that he did not, and could not, understand. So he contented himself with the company of politicians.

Shortly after Harold Wilson had retired from the premiership and left Downing Street, Goldsmith organized a private dinner for both Wilson and his predecessor in Downing Street, Edward Heath. 'I think it was the first time they had ever actually spent any time together alone and certainly it was the first time they had ever had dinner together without anyone else being present,' he has said. The dinner delighted him; it seemed to underline what he saw as his role in British politics, as he was the only other guest at the dinner. For it put him above the crowd, a friend and adviser of statesmen, rather than simply a multi-millionaire with a food business.

Indeed, he said later, 'The only political power I wanted was the power to influence ideas. Businessmen have nil power, they may think they have but they don't. But publishers have a little more power; and to be a publisher was a way of becoming a more committed, more participating observer.' He added, 'I do believe the press has a power, principally the power to destroy rather than to build.'

Perhaps with that in mind, he had had tentative discussions with Lord Barnetson, the chairman, in June to buy the humorous weekly magazine *Punch*. They had come to nothing. In any case, while the echoes of the argument over his knighthood continued to reverberate around Westminster and Whitehall there were other more important things to be done. Jimmy Goldsmith had heard of other accusations in the *Private Eye* case.

Two weeks before the announcement of his knighthood he had heard that Eric Levine was about to be discussed in the magazine again. Allegations about Levine's conduct while he was a member of the long-established firm of City solicitors, Leslie Paisner and Co, were about to be made.

Goldsmith had first heard about the allegations, which included the ill-founded suggestion of fraudulent conversion of money for an American client, at the end of April, and he had decided to see for himself both Leslie Paisner, whom he believed had made the accusations in the first place, and John Addey, a public relations man in the City of London with his own consultancy firm, who had also made them. On Thursday, 13 May, he had done so, and they had both repeated their allegations against Eric Levine. Goldsmith had immediately confronted Levine with the charges, but he denied them.

By Monday, 17 May, however, both Paisner and Addey had retracted their charges and sworn affidavits to that effect. It was a volte-face that neither Richard Ingrams nor Michael Gillard, who had been discussing the matter with John Addey, could understand.

As Goldsmith was to make clear in court three years later, 'I had every reason to believe that *Private Eye*, as part of their campaign, would try and publish these false allegations, or part of them, for an article about Eric Levine; and the trouble about these articles is that today it is possible to prove that they were all lies, but when they are made they do harm; and you have to be fairly strong to be able to subsist, to be able to live through such lies. Eric Levine, who had a comparatively young firm of solicitors, was worried about the permanent damage that it would do him. Therefore, in consultation with counsel, we decided to apply for proceedings to stop *Private Eye* publishing damaging articles about Eric Levine, only because he was my solicitor.'

On the day the *Daily Express* reported his peerage they also reported his return to the High Court the day before to seek a writ prohibiting 'Words, pictures or visual images tending to disparage or cast doubt on the private or personal integrity of Mr Eric Levine'. The change of heart by Addey and Paisner, which was later to form the basis of an action for slander and libel by Michael Gillard of *Private Eye* against Jimmy Goldsmith, was one of the least explained yet most significant, events in the strange history of the battle between the magazine and the financier, and it brought its casualties. Leslie Paisner retired from his successful firm within a matter of weeks of his change of heart, and he died not long afterwards. It had become a messy and bloody fight.

On the day of the retraction of the allegations against Levine, Goldsmith had telephoned the editors of *The Times*, the *Daily Telegraph*, the *Economist* and the *Sunday Express* and the proprietor of the *Spectator* to warn them that the allegations might still be made, and to warn them that one of *Private Eye*'s regular contributors, Michael Gillard, who was largely responsible for its 'Slicker' column on the dealings in the City of London, had been blackmailing John Addey. As he was to explain when the action for slander over those accusations came to court in June 1979, 'I felt it was therefore necessary to explain to the editors of leading newspapers what was happening and the gravity of their case, so that they looked more carefully at articles based on lies, appearing apparently independently in their paper but effectively part of the campaign of *Private Eye* to put pressure on me.' Subsequently he also repeated his allegations against Michael Gillard to one of the directors of Pressdram Limited (the company which published *Private Eye*), the publisher and author Anthony Blond whom he had known for years. Goldsmith intended to fight as vigorously as he could. No matter how brutal and imperious it may appear, if he were attacked, he would attack back; and in this case the counter-attack would finally bring him to court accused of slandering and libelling Michael Gillard.

So what had begun as an impetuous act (although he was later to deny it was) had become a time-consuming concern, and one which he rapidly realized would mean that he would remain for many years the subject of the most intense interest in the British press. For what Jimmy Goldsmith had not understood when he began was, as he admitted later, 'that the magazine was a club of British journalists and I did not realize the importance of what I was handling! I did not realize that *Private Eye* was part of the whole British press.' For a man who gave every appearance of understanding the world, it was a devastating naiveté. *Private Eye* had survived and prospered during its fifteen-year life by becoming the one publication many British journalists used to print anonymous stories that they could not convince their own newspapers or magazines to use. To attempt to crush it was to threaten the strain of iconoclasm and scepticism that lay at the heart of many British journalists. Goldsmith might have thought he could teach a small magazine a lesson but he found himself attacking almost the entire British press.

Certainly he had not realized that the case against *Private Eye* would fuel the persistent and bitter criticism of the announcement of his knighthood at the end of May. Richard Ingrams did, however. In his book on the case he wrote, 'There can be no doubt that a major cause of this upsurge of feeling against him was his campaign against *Private Eye*. It was mainly for this that he was well known. Until he sued *Private Eye*, Goldsmith was a relatively obscure figure.'

Nevertheless Jimmy Goldsmith was determined to fight on, more convinced than ever that he was not dealing simply with a magazine staffed by witty young men who revelled in the British taste for iconoclasm, but with one that had also become the tool of a small group of people with less engaging intentions.

He was also determined to keep on with his Acapulco plan gradually to remove his business to the United States. On the day Harold Wilson's resignation honours list was finally announced, he had attended an extraordinary general meeting of Cavenham in London to discuss the first stage of that withdrawal, the placing of Cavenham under the control of Générale Occidentale. Whatever else might be happening, that at least had still to proceed: and there seemed more sense in it now than ever as the publicity swirled about his head.

One unexpected benefit of the attacks on him in the British press had been to depress the share price of Cavenham. This allowed Sir James Goldsmith, as he had become, gradually to buy back his own shares at an exceptionally good price, which, as the court case came to an end, rose again in value. There are no firm estimates of how much the resulting transactions saved him, but a conservative estimate would not be far short of £50 million. The public price of the campaign against *Private Eye* had to be paid, but it had also brought this unanticipated financial benefit.

As the exceptionally hot summer of 1976 began, however, Goldsmith continued his attack on *Private Eye*. He spent the second week of July sitting in court for the first time, listening to the hearing before Mr Justice Donaldson of an injunction he had asked for on 18 May to prevent the magazine from mentioning Eric Levine in terms which Goldsmith contended were defamatory of him, and watching the cross-examination by his QC, Lewis Hawser, of Richard Ingrams, Auberon Waugh, Michael Gillard and Richard West whom he was accusing of a campaign of vilification against him. The cross-examination may have been enlightening, but Donaldson found against him on 16 July.

Undeterred, within a fortnight he was in court again, this time before the Chief Metropolitan Magistrate, Kenneth

Barraclough, at Bow Street to see Richard Ingrams face the serious charge of criminal libel.

Jimmy Goldsmith arrived at Bow Street with Annabel Birley. It was the first time they had been seen together so publicly, and it was a brave indication to everyone that she publicly supported him. She had come to see what was to be his sole appearance in the witness box during the battle with *Private Eye*. Not until three years later, during the slander case against him, would he again give evidence in person. As he told a slightly mystified Kenneth Barraclough that morning, 'Until this case I think I had only issued one writ for libel in my life.' Hardly anyone in the tiny crowded court room could believe it. In only six months his name had become synonymous with libel.

To the surprise of some who packed the courtroom, Goldsmith seemed remarkably agitated. He paced up and down the small witness box while presenting his evidence, gesticulating as he always did, occasionally bringing his fist down hard on the rail around him to give emphasis. He was hardly an orthodox witness. Yet it was not a calculated performance. He had always been prone to pace when he was excited, just as he had a tendency to bite his handkerchief, and he had always waved his arms to make a point. An astonished magistrate asked him if he would mind behaving 'a little less theatrically'. Rather taken aback, the French-born Jimmy Goldsmith replied, 'I am sorry, I find it difficult to keep still.'

As he left the courtroom, to Annabel Birley's congratulations, the *Evening Standard* front-page headline read, 'Goldsmith tells criminal libel hearing, "I'm not trying to smash the *Eye*".' He had told James Comyn, who appeared for the magazine, that he had already tried to reach a generous settlement with them which would allow the magazine to survive intact 'although perhaps a little more truthfully', and he had also told the court that the proceedings were the result of 'the campaign against me fortnight after fortnight'. He went on, 'I occupy a position of public prominence and trust, being responsible for managing the investments of more than 300,000 people. *Private Eye* has mounted a campaign to undermine that position.'

The Chief Metropolitan Magistrate did indeed give permission for the case for criminal libel to go ahead, in spite of the serious reservations raised about it by Lord Shawcross and others in a letter to *The Times* after Mr Justice Wien's original decision in April and the subsequent refusal of the Director of Public Prosecutions to take over the case. Jimmy Goldsmith had won the first round, but the price had been very high. He had made an enormous number of enemies whom he had never met, but who were nevertheless convinced he represented a force to be condemned, a force which was intent on manipulating English society. Appearance or reality, it would never be forgotten.

By now the campaign against *Private Eye* had become an obsession. The fight that he had begun in January, when he had not known what to do, had become a crusade. He was determined to use whatever means he could to put an end to the campaign of vilification, as he kept on describing it, and at the same time to stand up for all those who had ever been attacked by *Private Eye*. Encouraged by a great many who never had the courage to admit their support for him openly, it was a stand which divided those who observed it. He was either an admirable defender of the *Eye*'s victims or a tyrant who deserved to be despised for attempting to crush it. No other explanation would do. For most people his determination seemed a tyrant's obsession. Why else would he instruct his solicitors to brief a firm of private investigators to search through *Private Eye*'s dustbins in pursuit of evidence to support his case? Why else would he encourage them to follow and photograph leading members of the *Eye*'s journalists, including Richard Ingrams and Nigel Dempster?

It seemed the action of an obsessive somehow hardly balanced man who was determined to win at whatever cost, and determined to use every means at his disposal to do so. He defended it later by saying, 'I felt they were attacking me with everything they could, and I decided to fight back with everything I could. I had to find out whether this was in fact co-ordinated or whether it was my imagination. That is why I took private detectives to find out who really worked for *Private Eye*. This produced a

149

substantial list and confirmed what I had suspected.' His action nevertheless offended the English sense of fair play. Yet again he had not played by the English rules. When his use of private detectives in this way was finally revealed in court by Lewis Hawser QC during the next criminal libel hearing in the case – early in August, barely seven days after the hearing at Bow Street – it only served further to convince those already sceptical of him of his vengeful streak. The polarization of opinion about him was almost complete.

Shortly after the Bow Street hearing of the criminal libel case Jimmy Goldsmith left for a holiday in Corsica, aware that the man who had helped him create not only Cavenham, but also Générale Occidentale and Anglo-Continental Investments, his cousin Baron Alexis de Gunzburg, had decided to resign. Not as the *Daily Telegraph* had reported, 'following personal disagreements between himself and Sir James', but for 'personal reasons' of his own, as he had told the *Daily Telegraph* himself later. It was the end of a business partnership which had lasted a dozen years and seen the foundation of a commercial empire which now employed 66,000 people around the world and had pre-tax profits in 1975–6 of £34·7 million. Goldsmith's brief chairman's statement for the financial year ending in March 1976 pointed out, 'Cavenham has now completed the first two major phases of its development ... We are now ready to embark on the third phase. This will be based on a programme of major capital investment in our mainstream activities, and our present plans are to invest in excess of £200 million in the next five years.'

Before the end of his Corsican holiday, however, *Private Eye* had returned to the attack, with an article about Leslie Paisner and John Addey's change of heart and their resulting affidavits, in which they admitted misleading others. Entitled 'The Erasing of Lazarus' (Leslie Paisner's middle name was Lazarus), it too was to become the subject of a contempt of court proceeding, although not until October. Before then, however, there were other important matters for Goldsmith to attend to, the difficulties of Slater Walker.

*

On Wednesday, 15 September, with the case against *Private Eye* temporarily out of the headlines, the first complete report on Slater Walker's Securities was published. Within hours the company's share price had fallen from 16 pence to 8 pence, for a share which had once stood on the London Stock Market at £3.30. A few days later, on 23 September, fifteen summonses alleging breaches of Section 54 of the Companies Act were issued by the Department of Trade and Industry against Jim Slater for the conduct of the company before Goldsmith had arrived as chairman. On the following day the Singapore Government asked for the extradition of Jim Slater, Dick Tarling and three other Slater Walker men on charges of fraud and conspiracy.

Barely two weeks later Jimmy Goldsmith found himself explaining to the stormy annual general meeting of Slater Walker Securities that 'without the support of the Bank of England Slater Walker would not have been able to keep trading'. Altogether the Bank had made available £110 million to keep the company operating, and while the reorganization that Jimmy Goldsmith had conceived with the help of his fellow directors had been put into effect, and the Haw Par issue 'closed', not much credit was attached to his achievements in the reports of the meeting or of Slater Walker's difficulties. The shareholders were happy enough with their chairman's performance, but a group of demonstrators, who started shouting slogans at him, were not. They were finally ejected, and two of the counter-attackers were John Aspinall's mother Lady Osborne, and Jimmy Goldsmith's own mother who attacked them with their umbrellas. Goldsmith may have become a familiar figure in the headlines, but since the *Private Eye* case had begun he had not appeared too often as a saviour. Indeed throughout his period as chairman his achievements at Slater Walker were to be almost submerged beneath the publicity for his battle against *Private Eye*.

Predictably it was not Slater Walker that brought him back into the headlines as October drew on, but nor was it simply the hearing of a further action for contempt of court which he had brought against *Private Eye*. This time there was a new reason for the attention. The possibility had emerged that he might be able to become a newspaper publisher. His principal business interests would be elsewhere but it might be an interesting hobby. It might even provide a platform from which to attack those who had attacked him.

The *Observer*, Britain's oldest Sunday newspaper, was in dire financial straits, its circulation was falling, and as the Astor family, one of whom, David Astor, had edited it with great distinction for almost thirty years until 1975, had decided to give up the financial battle to sustain the paper, he and The Observer Trust which controlled it, were considering to whom it might be sold. The chairman of the paper's Trust was Lord Goodman.

There have been a number of versions of what happened, including an interesting one in Lewis Chester and Jonathan Fenby's admirable book, *The Fall of the House of Beaverbrook*, but Jimmy Goldsmith's account of the events has never been completely reported. He said later, 'One morning I was reading an article in the *Daily Mail* about Rupert Murdoch's interest in the *Observer*. It was breakfast time. In the article I read that Lord Goodman had stated that I would definitely not get the *Observer* and that I would be repelled. I was amazed by this as I had made no advances and therefore I wondered how I could be repelled. So then I telephoned Goodman at his home. He told me he had been misquoted. He said that David Astor and the paper's managing director were about to have breakfast with him and would I like to join them. I did so. They asked me whether I would be interested and I said yes. They then asked me whether I would guarantee editorial independence. I said no.

Excited by the prospect, but still a businessman, Jimmy Goldsmith made it clear to the Trust that he was simply exploring the possibilities that might exist. He admitted that he wanted to be a publisher.

Jimmy Goldsmith's plan for the *Observer* involved the transfer of its printing to the new Beaverbrook presses in Fleet Street. He had come up with this scheme after consultation with his contemporary at Eton, Jocelyn Stevens, the deputy chairman and managing director of the Beaverbrook Group of newspapers which included the *Daily* and *Sunday Express* as well as the London *Evening Standard*.

'After studying the facts and figures,' Jimmy Goldsmith remembers today, 'it was clear to me that the *Observer* could never be viable so long as it was both an industrial and publishing business. I felt that the printing works had to be closed and the company had to revert to its old structure of being purely publishers with somebody else printing for them'. It was after he had been convinced of that necessity that he had discussed with Stevens and Beaverbrook the possibility that he might put money into their company. 'With this money Beaverbrook would buy the *Observer*.'

Goldsmith then intended that the publishing side of the *Observer* should be put into a new subsidiary of Beaverbrook, and he would be chairman and in charge of this new subsidiary. 'Beaverbrook would print the *Observer* as they had the spare industrial capacity. What is more they had just completed an office building in Fleet Street and the *Observer* would move into these offices next to Beaverbrook.' The plan's final element was that he would join the main Beaverbrook board.

Before he was prepared to take his plans any further, Jimmy Goldsmith asked to meet some of the senior editorial staff of the *Observer*. He wanted to assess their reaction; for their part, they wanted to see, in the words of one who met him, 'whether or not blood dripped off his fangs'. He invited them to dinner at his house in Tregunter Road, and while the discussions went on, to the consternation of several of them, before each of their places the butler placed a bottle of claret. The effect on the attitude of the journalists present was, they recalled later, considerable. Some felt as though they were being treated as drunks. As far as Jimmy Goldsmith was concerned it was simply a generous gesture, the sort he would have made to a friend at dinner, but once again he had failed to grasp the puritan ethic at work in many journalists, no matter what licentious public image they may present.

One of the *Observer* journalists at the dinner, Michael Davie, reported shrewdly not long afterwards, 'Even if

Goldsmith were interested in the routes to political power, of which he has never shown any sign, they are not open to him. Yet he wants power. Ergo, the obvious step is into publishing. He did not conceal, in his dealings with us, that he would want a say in *Observer* policy ... But he claimed – most persuasively, since he is nothing if not persuasive – that he would always attempt to get his views across by reasoned argument, not by diktat. He would never be another Beaverbrook or Northcliffe. He would never give orders about editorial content ... To impose his opinions on us would be hopeless, he said.'

Not all the paper's journalists, however, were convinced.

Certainly Jimmy Goldsmith's appeal as a potential proprietor of the *Observer* to its journalists was not helped by his return to court in his battle against *Private Eye* at the end of October. Angry this time at the magazine's report of the Paisner case on 28 August, he had again asked for Richard Ingrams to be charged with contempt of court. It was the second time within a little over three months that he had brought such an action. On the previous occasion Mr Justice Donaldson had noted tartly, 'These proceedings should not have been brought in the manner they were brought,' and although he had not had Ingrams sent to prison for contempt, he had fined him £250.

Yet there were some consolations. On the day his contempt hearing was due to begin in the High Court he had been to Buckingham Palace to be dubbed a knight by the Queen for his 'services to export and ecology'. It was a citation which many found difficult to understand, but his friend Sam White, the *Evening Standard*'s Paris correspondent, explained it as an oblique reference by Sir Harold Wilson to his action against the 'pollution' of *Private Eye*. That theory was later supported by Richard Ingrams who reported that White had suggested as a humorous aside that the honour was intended both as a reward and to give him a higher standing with society.

For his part Goldsmith simply said later that he believed his knighthood was 'at least partly' for his services to ecology: he had helped to fund the Ecological Foundation and had supported the Friends of the Earth with a £25,000 donation for their opposition to British Nuclear Fuels expansion of the Windscale Nuclear Power plant. 'I felt that the opposition had very little finance, and that if they could not put their case forward they would be forced into the streets.' He himself was opposed to nuclear energy – though not to nuclear defence. In fact, it is possible that the award was designed to give him a higher standing, but in Slater Walker and the City of London as much as against *Private Eye*.

Nonetheless, no sooner had he left Buckingham Palace than he was in court to hear Lewis Hawser QC once again accuse *Private Eye* of a 'campaign of vilification' against him. He told the court in a written statement, 'It is in this way that the editor and contributors of *Private Eye* have combined to create and maintain a climate in which it will be difficult for there to be a fair trial of my legal proceedings.'

The Lord Chief Justice, Lord Widgery, was not impressed. Sitting with Mr Justice Eveleigh and Mr Justice Peter Pain, he found that even if there had been intent on *Private Eye*'s part to do something which was contempt of court, that intent in itself was not enough to establish contempt as the law defined it. He added that he did not feel the article 'The Erasing of Lazarus' would give rise to a real risk of a prejudicial effect on a fair and proper trial of future proceedings. Goldsmith had lost, and found himself having to pay an estimated £8,000 in costs for the case.

The following day Richard Ingrams accused him of being 'determined to crush' his magazine and suggested that John Addey and Leslie Paisner had sworn their affidavits under some sort of pressure. It seemed to some, and certainly to some of the *Observer* journalists he had been trying to reassure, that Goldsmith was indeed intent on trying to destroy the fortnightly magazine that some of them privately supported. It was not the behaviour they expected of a proprietor of a great Sunday newspaper proud of its liberal traditions. Any hopes he may have had for the *Observer* had begun to dim.

By now even the *New York Times* had begun to take interest in the case. The newspaper described it as 'One of Britain's most interesting legal battles – interesting not only because of the issues involved but also the personalities involved.' The paper added that Jimmy Goldsmith openly led a multi-national family life with 'wife in Paris, a companion in London and children by both', and described *Private Eye* as being powered by 'contempt for big shots of any description'.

The two contempt of court actions during the summer, coming in the midst of his criminal libel action, convinced most disinterested observers of the case that Jimmy Goldsmith was indeed determined to see Richard Ingrams sent to prison for his editorship of *Private Eye*. Whether this were true or not, and in all probability during that summer it was true, it ensured Jimmy Goldsmith of a public reputation in England for vengefulness. Richard Ingrams might joke with the *Daily Mail* before the first contempt case that he had been to have a haircut before the hearing in case he was sent to jail, adding, 'I didn't want the State barber to get at me,' but that only further convinced the British public that here was the victim of a rich and powerful financier with an obsession. Mistaken or not, and whatever the reasons for his taking up the battle in the first place, that impression was finally to put an end to Jimmy Goldsmith's liking for the country of his father's birth.

Throughout the battle, however, Goldsmith maintained a steadfast public silence about what he felt, and what forces he believed had to be overthrown. At no stage did he try to alter the growing public conception of him as an obsessive financier. It was certainly not the reaction of a man carefully preparing his political ambitions, or the response of a man who saw his entire future in England, it was rather the behaviour of someone who had always been determined to win, and who had always been convinced he was right. The end justified the means, no matter what anyone else may think. An opportunity to explain would present itself later, perhaps then there would be a chance to explain who he was attacking and who supported him. Until then, let it remain a mystery.

By the end of the second contempt of court hearing, Rupert Murdoch had reached the brink of agreement with the *Observer* Trust. But then suddenly the paper was sold to the American oil company, Atlantic Richfield (ARCO), after a dinner at Rules between Kenneth Harris, an *Observer* writer, and Douglas Cater, an ARCO adviser. Their ownership was to last less than five years, but Goldsmith had never even made a bid for the paper, in spite of the widespread conviction that he had. Indeed he was so convinced that his plan for the integration of the paper into Beaverbrook would only work as a last resort, that he had gone on holiday to Mexico to a place where there was not even a telephone.

When he got back to New York in November to see the Grand Union part of Cavenham, a trip he had been making more and more regularly in the previous two years, Jimmy Goldsmith discovered that ARCO had bought the *Observer* and met Rupert Murdoch. The Australian newspaper tycoon, who had just bought the *New York Post*, offered to sell him the holding he had built up in Beaverbrook newspapers. He accepted. Ironically, this was not the first time he had been offered this block of 4,400,000 Beaverbrook A shares. Only a year or so earlier Lady Annabel Birley's brother-in-law, then still Sir Max Rayne, had offered them to him, but he had turned them down. Instead, Rayne sold them back to Rupert Murdoch who had sold them to him in the first place four years before that. Rayne had offered them to Goldsmith at a good price but at that time he had no intention of becoming a publisher. After the *Observer* negotiations, however, things had changed. As the *Economist* was to note a few months later, 'Sir James Goldsmith is an exceedingly old-fashioned sort of man. Having made his pile he wants to become a press tycoon.'

In fact he had also started contemplating becoming a publisher in both France and the United States. The owner and publisher of *New York* magazine, Clay Felker, had already discussed the possibility of his buying his magazine, together with the two others in his stable, *New West* and the *Village Voice*, just as later he was to discuss buying *Esquire* with him; but the deals never came off. But he had also been conducting quiet negotiations to buy the French weekly news magazine *L'Express* from its politician owner, Jean Jacques Servan-Schrieber. Those negotiations were a good deal more successful.

There was another, less obvious reason why Jimmy Goldsmith bought Rupert Murdoch's Beaverbrook shares, and that was associated with *Private Eye*. He bought them to keep them out of the hands of Vere Harmsworth, the proprietor of Associated Newspapers and owner of Beaverbrook's principal daily newspaper rival, the *Daily Mail*. He did it, he was to say later, 'as a financial penalty for Nigel Dempster', whom he saw not only as a collaborator with *Private Eye* but also as the regular reporter of his private life in his gossip column. Indeed, his dislike of Dempster's reporting was to remain in his mind, and he later expressed his dislike to Vere Harmsworth, the grandson of the first Lord Rothermere who, with his brilliant but eccentric brother Lord Northclife, had created the British popular press with the *Daily Mail*. Not long afterwards Harmsworth was to convey his own reservations about Dempster to the *Daily Mail*'s editor, comparing his column to 'cold fried potatoes'.

It was not until the beginning of 1977, however, and the launch of the Beaverbrook-sponsored Boat Show in London on 11 January, that Goldsmith made his Beaverbrook shares public. By then he had increased his holding to nearly 5 million A shares, about 35 per cent of the total. But because of the structure of Beaverbrook newspapers, this gave him no formal power whatsoever in the company's affairs. That remained with the voting shares, which were primarily in the hands of the Beaverbrook family under the leadership of the late Lord Beaverbrook's son, Sir Max Aitken. Now Jimmy Goldsmith may have been a friend of Jocelyn Stevens, just as his own father had been a friend of the late Lord Beaverbrook, but he was emphatically not a friend of Sir Max Aitken.

As Chester and Fenby wrote later, 'Sir Max Aitken, as it turned out, was not in the least amused.' Indeed, the strength of his reaction against him surprised even Goldsmith himself. Certainly Sir Max Aitken cherished the advice of Lord Goodman, his 'passive enemy' during the *Observer* take-over discussion, and as the Beaverbrook discussions developed he became, as Jimmy Goldsmith suspected Lord Goodman had become, a more 'active' enemy. Within a few days Sir Max Aitken had made it extremely clear that he had no wish to see his newspapers fall into the hands of Sir James Goldsmith, and that seemed to have nothing to do with his litigation against *Private Eye*. It was an opposition he could not combat. By 23 January, Goldsmith had told everyone concerned that he would not push any further into Beaverbrook without Sir Max Aitken's blessing, and the possibility of his assuming the mantle of Lord Beaverbrook as a press baron had again become extremely remote.

But it was not the question of becoming a publisher that preoccupied Jimmy Goldsmith most at the beginning of 1977, nor indeed his continuing battle with *Private Eye*; it was his desire to escape from the public eye. On Friday, 28 January, only a few days after he had made it clear he would not press into Beaverbrook, he had begun a process that would lead to his no longer being chairman of Cavenham. As he put it, 'I can't say I've enjoyed it. I've disliked it. Not much is done to make things enjoyable for chairmen of public companies. They tend to be targets and I see no reason why they should put up with it.' He was not only intending to get out, however, he was also announcing his intention to buy out the remaining 44 per cent of Cavenham that was still in public hands. 'Now we are very much following a policy that we should paddle our own canoe in private,' he added.

To those who had often accused him of seeking the limelight it seemed a peculiar decision, but further evidence of his secretiveness. Even the *Economist* reported, 'He has suffered, he says, twelve years of virtually unmitigated press vilification, despite being responsible for one of Britain's post-war industrial success stories: and nobody, least of all the stock market, understands him.' For Jimmy Goldsmith had decided to acknowledge not only that he would always be an outsider, but also that he wanted to remain one.

Consequently, after a brief suspension of dealings on the Stock Exchange, Générale Occidentale bid 120 pence a share for Cavenham shares. The move was not greeted with enthusiasm by the City establishment. As some of the bid's critics pointed out, in 1973 Cavenham's shares had stood at 230 pence. Gradually, over the next few weeks, it became clear that Jimmy Goldsmith was not going to be able to remove himself from England quite as easily as he had planned. In the middle of March from Barbados, he simply rang up Peter Hill-Wood of Hambros and told him the deal was off. What the City of London did not know was that he did not intend to be put off the idea for long.

While his GO bid for Cavenham was temporarily stuck, Jimmy Goldsmith had won a victory over *Private Eye*. An appeal against the string of libel writs he had issued against *Private Eye* and its distributors had been rejected by the Court of Appeal sitting under Lord Denning, the Master of the Rolls. Even though Denning himself remarked, 'No private individual should be allowed to stifle a publication by suing its distributors for libel. ... The freedom of the press depends on the channels of distribution being kept open,' and Lord Scarman, sitting with him, added, 'Neither wealth nor power entitles a man to censor the press,' the court ruled by two to one that he could go ahead. The magazine admitted during the week-long hearing that it had lost 12,000 sales every fortnight as a result of the action, and that its legal costs so far had amounted to £30,000 or more. Lord Denning (the dissenting judge) may have seemed to vindicate *Private Eye* but the magazine had still lost.

There was another victory for Jimmy Goldsmith to celebrate that month. On 16 March 1977 he finally succeeded in becoming a publisher. Through his Agrifurane subsidiary in France, itself a subsidiary of Générale Alimentaire and therefore of Cavenham, he paid £3·5m for 45 per cent of Groupe Express, the publishers of *L'Express*, the biggest weekly news magazine in France with 550,000 copies sold every week. Founded in 1953, it had even been a daily paper for eleven years of its history between 1955 and 1966, and had always had a strong left-wing and radical tradition. Not everyone liked the purchase; *Le Matin* commented, 'A paper which ceases to belong to its founder, journalists sold like part of the furniture – it is more than sad – it is serious.' But Goldsmith had got the 'voice' in the public debate that he had so often talked about over the past few months, yet he did not begin to use it to promulgate his own opinions. Instead he ran it as a business which had to stand on its own feet. Publisher he might be, but he was not a philanthropist, he was a businessman. News magazines, like jam, sugar mice or supermarkets had to make money – or at least not lose too much. Within a comparatively short time even his critics were to admit that *L'Express* had not lost its radical voice in the hands of a proprietor who had a reputation in Britain for such staunchly right-wing opinions. He told Edward Behr of *Newsweek*, '*L'Express* is a news magazine and as such it should report objectively. Anyone's individual views should not come through too strongly. Editorially, my own feeling is that there must be access to a broad spectrum of political thought – not the most extreme ones perhaps – and that's what will happen.' He went on to say, 'Not only do I believe in a vigorous and free press but I would fight for it as an absolute necessity, as an element in protecting the way of life we wish to see preserved.'

He added later, 'When I acquired *L'Express* I realized I was acquiring an institution. To be the real owner of a newspaper you should create it. Even though I made it quite clear that I had no intention of not interfering with the editorial content – indeed I chaired many editorial meetings in the first few months – I felt within myself that my role was more of an arbiter. I saw my job as getting the right people into the paper and ensuring that it respected the highest possible standards of journalism'.

Jimmy Goldsmith resolved to interfere when he felt he had to, because 'there was absolutely no way I would be willing to be associated with a newspaper whose editorial line was one that I considered evil or destructive and that would by my position no matter what the commercial success or profitability of that paper might be.' He also remarked, 'Unfortunately some people use our respect for the freedom of the press as a screen behind which they can work to transform our society into one which would no longer tolerate this basic and vital freedom. Many of these people are backed by slush funds whose purpose is to encourage subversion in our community.'

Jimmy Goldsmith had become a publisher, and although

several newspapers in England speculated that he had the foundation of a triangular publishing empire with newspapers or magazines in France, Britain and America in his mind, they could not have known the opportunity to establish a British leg would come so quickly.

11. The *Express* Train

In the spring air of April 1977 the magnificent if rather sedate Georgian mansion, Ormeley Lodge, which looks out over the bushes and small trees of Ham Common, with the taller brooding oaks of Richmond Park behind it, showed unusual signs of activity. The garden, with its tennis court and swimming pool, looked as though it had recently been cleaned and tidied, in preparation for a summer's visitors, while inside the house was abustle everywhere from the bathrooms to the pantries.

Lady Annabel Birley and her interior decorator were transforming the house from the plain style of its previous owner, Lord Howard de Walden, into something a little prettier, and distinctly more patterned. Upstairs a nursery was being created for Lady Annabel's two youngest children, Jemima and Zacharias, and downstairs in the basement a room big enough to entertain a hundred guests in comfort was being wallpapered. There was a faint hint of chinoiserie, but the predominant style was Queen Anne by way of Chelsea. The sofas were often cream, the wallpaper pink or brown.

Behind the tall iron gates that surrounded its courtyard and steps up to the front door a family house was being refurbished, which Lady Annabel Birley's young children would call home, even if their father was not always there.

Jimmy Goldsmith had never really had a permanent home, and he had not missed it. The nomadic ways of a childhood spent in hotel suites had never entirely left him. Still, he appeared to enjoy the new house take shape more than some of his friends had expected, and it clearly delighted Annabel. 'It is an old Jewish trait', a friend said later, 'to want to be with your family when you can, and Jimmy had not escaped it.' Besides, he had not entirely given up hope of having more children; Annabel had already had one miscarriage since Zacharias's birth fifteen months earlier.

Ormeley Lodge, however, was not to be his permanent home. For tax-saving purposes, and to suit his own taste for living in a series of compartments, he remained officially domiciled in France. He preferred to insulate himself in his own private world, away from England, wary in case of attack from enemies he did not know. Since the *Private Eye* case had started fifteen months before, his friends had begun to notice a change in him. He had become a little harder, a little less relaxed. His chauffeur had taken advanced driving courses to avoid kidnappers or assassins, his security advisers were considering how best to protect his new home. Whether or not it was an exaggerated feeling, Jimmy Goldsmith felt he was under siege in England, with no respite from the attentions of the press, no hiding from the abuse of people who believed he was a tyrant or a demagogue (even though the vast majority of the letters he received supported him) and this had its effect on his family. There had even been the occasional bogus threat at his offices, although no one took them particularly seriously. Nevertheless, he had become deliberately, permanently secretive about his life and his intentions, and extremely protective of his family.

The only place he seemed to feel free to do what he chose with whom he chose, when he wanted to, was in the United States where he was unknown, and content to remain so. In England that was impossible, and it was even becoming difficult in France. Ormeley Lodge had to be made into a fortress for him so that behind its high iron railings and brick garden walls he could not be spied upon.

One ambition in particular remained to be properly satisfied: to establish some kind of political influence. To remind those who doubted him or criticized him that he was as entitled as they were to have his own opinions: and he was rich enough to ensure that opinions of all kinds could be promulgated. He no longer sought political power, but influence was quite another matter, and he knew that if he owned a newspaper or a magazine that would deliver the influence.

So when he received a telephone call soon after lunch on Wednesday 27 April at his office in Leadenhall Street in the City of London from Charles Wintour, managing director of the *Daily Express* and a director of Express Newspapers, he did not hesitate. He invited him round to tea.

By midnight on the following day, after reaching an agreement with his old friend Jocelyn Stevens, Goldsmith had made it clear to everyone at Express newspapers, from the proprietor, Sir Max Aitken, to the printing unions and the journalists, and to the government, that he was seriously interested in injecting money into the group to save the London *Evening Standard* from a planned merger with its traditional rival, London's only other evening newspaper, the *Evening News*.

Everything had been done at breakneck pace because the *Evening News*'s owners, Associated Newspapers, had already planned to announce on Thursday, 28 April, their agreement to take over the *Evening Standard*. They had even called a meeting to explain the result of their negotiations with the group created by Lord Beaverbrook, the *Standard*'s owners. When Jocelyn Stevens told the assembled crowd of printers, journalists and management at the Bonnington Hotel that the takeover was off because there had been a last minute intervention by Jimmy Goldsmith, there was a stunned silence. In the words of Chester and Fenby's book, 'Lord Goodman looked stunned, Harmsworth looked rueful.' Goldsmith's old adversary Lord Goodman had been advising Vere Harmsworth, Associated Newspaper's proprietor on his takeover of the *Standard*.

Yet no matter how it may have appeared to the television audience that night who heard he was interested in helping to save the *Standard*, Jimmy Goldsmith could not do exactly what he chose with Cavenham's money – for it was Cavenham, not he, that owned 37 per cent of Beaverbrook's non-voting A shares, recently acquired from Rupert Murdoch. He might aspire to Lord Beaverbrook's mantle as a press lord, and he seemed rich enough to put it on, but there were other more complicated issues to be settled. He had spent thirteen years creating the Cavenham group, and that was not to be ignored lightly.

So Jimmy Goldsmith had not simply taken out his chequebook and written a cheque to buy Beaverbrook newspapers. As he was to say later, 'You cannot buy a company merely by buying its shares.' In any case there were no voting rights or management responsibilities attached to his shareholding. All he had said publicly was that he would like to look at the possibility of injecting money into the newspaper group in exchange for some kind of role in running it; and that he wanted six weeks to consider the best way of doing it.

Within a couple of days, however, he had come up with a simple scheme, which offered to keep the *Evening Standard* alive in return for his being involved in Beaverbrook management: He would guarantee the group's debts in return for the enfranchisement of his shares. It was not the only offer that Beaverbrook received now that their first negotiations with Associated had fallen through, but then Jimmy Goldsmith had not yet refined a strategy for owning newspapers in the way that he had for developments in every other area of his business life.

Although his original proposal in February that GO should take over Cavenham, thereby allowing him to 'paddle his own canoe', had been turned down in Britain and had met opposition from one of his larger shareholders, the massive Prudential Assurance Company, the scheme was still very much in his mind. He knew that an outright bid by Cavenham for Beaverbrook would not tally with that plan, which he had been nurturing for more than four years. As Chester and Fenby accurately reported, 'Purchase of Beaverbrook Newspapers might be viewed as fundamentally changing the nature of Cavenham and his capital raising operation could be compromised as a result. Whereas if buying Beaverbrook brought down his share price, because it was hardly the profitable operation that *L'Express* was in France, then his shareholders might accuse him of using the acquisition to buy Cavenham shares more cheaply than he would otherwise have done.' So Jimmy Goldsmith did not plunge into the fray at Express Newspapers as a potential proprietor desperate to get his hands on a famous publishing empire. Instead he hovered on the edge of affairs. Then, finally, he entered the bidding properly, but only in conjunction with a man he hardly knew, and whom he had not come to like,

Roland 'Tiny' Rowland, whom Edward Heath once described as 'the unacceptable face of capitalism'.

Goldsmith had hardly met 'Tiny' Rowland. Indeed he only telephoned him about the *Standard* and the *Express* deal after Vere Harmsworth had asked him whether he knew what Rowland's intentions were. He agreed to find out.

In the next few weeks these two unlikely partners launched a bid for Express newspapers, only to fail ultimately amidst a welter of bitter accusations against one another. Jimmy Goldsmith claimed 'Tiny' Rowland had disappeared at the crucial moment, while Rowland reportedly claimed that Jimmy Goldsmith could not come up with the money he had promised. One factor that certainly did not lead to harmony between the joint bidders was that Rowland had donated £5000 to the *Private Eye* 'Goldenballs' libel fund, which the magazine had created to help pay for their defence.

'But I went on with the partnership,' Jimmy Goldsmith said later, 'partly because I wanted to stop "Tiny" getting complete control of the papers. I thought that might not turn out to be a very good thing.'

In fact the *Private Eye* case was an obstacle to a man who appeared to have an interest, albeit a rather uncertain one, in owning a Beaverbrook newspaper. His dispute with that magazine had already cost Jimmy Goldsmith dearly in his preliminary discussions over the *Observer* by alienating some journalists, and he had begun to realize that it might again prove decisive by having a similar impact on the Express journalists. The only benefit it had brought him was to encourage the City's more traditional investment managers to sell their holdings in Cavenham and thereby help his plans to put the company under GO. Jocelyn Stevens had been urging him to settle the *Private Eye* dispute out of court, as had Charles Wintour, now his staunch supporter at the Express group; but more significantly, so had Madame Beaux.

So, a little reluctantly, in the first week of May Goldsmith decided to call off his criminal libel proceedings against *Private Eye*. As he put it later, 'The criminal libel had been a tactical mistake in any case.'

After a rapid series of negotiations organized by the *Evening Standard*'s recently appointed young editor Simon Jenkins, it was agreed that a full-page apology from *Private Eye* to Jimmy Goldsmith would be printed in the *Evening Standard*. The magazine also agreed to contribute £30,000 towards his costs, to be paid in annual instalments over the next ten years.

When Richard Ingrams left the dock at the Old Bailey only ten days later, after Lewis Hawser QC had explained to Mr Justice Bridge that the case had been settled, he said, 'I left with the strong conviction that we would have lost the case.'

Jimmy Goldsmith himself said later, 'I regret the settlement.' He did not feel that he had explained his case sufficiently, and he believed that the libel case should have continued. The only mistake, he accepted, had been to press for criminal libel. 'That was a poor decision,' he said.

The dispute's unsatisfactory, truncated ending resolved none of the bitterness it had created. Nevertheless, Goldsmith told the *Sunday Telegraph* a few days later, 'As far as I am concerned *Private Eye* is past history,' and went on to say that he wanted to become involved in the newspaper industry because it was 'creative, amusing, challenging – that's the extra dimension. The extra dimension means a lot to me.' But when asked exactly why he was doing it he could only answer, 'The male menopause.' It was hardly the style of financial dealing that was typical of Cavenham or of him, it sounded altogether too much like a whim, the same whim that had taken him out of the battle against *Private Eye*. It was a whim he would regret.

After the *Eye* case was closed – though before the slander action brought against him by Michael Gillard was settled – Jimmy Goldsmith invited Richard Ingrams to come and see him; but even then the two men were destined never to meet. 'My wife did not want me to go and meet the man,' Ingrams has said, 'so I didn't, although in a way I wish I had.'

Private Eye's apology for its libel, worded by Goldsmith's lawyers and printed in the *Evening Standard* included the sentences, '*Private Eye* accepts that Sir James would have been entitled to very substantial damages for what *Private Eye* said about him. He has, however, made it clear that our unreserved apology will satisfy him and he has waived his right to damages,' and 'It has never been the intention of *Private Eye* to pursue any personal or public vendetta against Sir James Goldsmith and he has our sincere assurance that we will not do so in future issues of *Private Eye*.' But his victory was still sour: nothing had been resolved, and, worse, it was to haunt his public reputation.

Three days after the apology was printed, Goldsmith went back to his principal interest – withdrawing from England. He announced that Générale Occidentale was returning to the British Stock Market with an improved offer of £80 million for the minority he did not own in Cavenham. By the middle of June his move had been completed, and so had a simultaneous merger of Cavenham and Grand Union in the United States. Things had finally gone according to plan.

But his joint offer with 'Tiny' Rowland for the Beaverbrook group had not. Sir Max Aitken's implacable opposition to him had effectively squashed any serious consideration of the plan he had proposed to enfranchise his non-voting A shares. Meanwhile both Nigel Broakes of Trafalgar House and Rupert Murdoch had thrown their hats into the ring as other possible owners for the newspapers. The ultimately successful Broakes had been brought into it by another scion of a Frankfurt banking family, Evelyn de Rothschild. To get involved in a full-scale battle with Trafalgar House for all three Beaverbrook newspapers Jimmy Goldsmith would have to match their £13·69 million bid. He thought that price was too high.

He drew some small consolation, however, from the non-voting shares he had bought from Rupert Murdoch six months earlier which were sold to Trafalgar House at the end of July for almost £4 million. It was a profit of more than £2 million.

He had already begun to consider the possibility of starting his own weekly news magazine in England. If he did that there would be no need to consult with any existing proprietor, he could avoid the pitfalls of negotiations with the powerful Fleet Street printing unions, he could use the latest technology, and he could make sure no single printer could hold him to ransom by halting production. He could employ a group of printing firms rather than one.

Within a few months he was telling *The Times*: 'I am definitely going to be in the newspaper industry in Britain within a reasonably short-term future.' But he went on to explain, 'First I want to complete my task of reorganizing *L'Express*, which is a thoroughly profitable paper, to learn a little more about what I am doing ... When I feel confident we will come here one way or the other. I can assure you that we will be here.' It was almost two years, however, before this came about.

In the meantime there were a number of other, rather more commercially significant things to be done: among them selling Cavenham's Générale Alimentaire subsidiary to Générale Occidentale to avoid paying tax on its profits in France twice, and of course in the process to continue to remove himself from the chairmanship of a British company. Jimmy Goldsmith had said before, 'The chairman of a public company in Britain must be either a masochist or a fool. I am neither.'

The man who believed he had always had an ability to think strategically about financial movements, and the world's economic future, and believed his record of commercial success proved that ability, had evolved an explanation for his treatment in Britain. He had been misunderstood. He had been criticized for not taking kindly to the British habit of pragmatism, their tradition of the expedient response to any difficulty. That was why the City of London had misunderstood him, and why the British press had suspected him. They were not accustomed to his train of thought, or to his belief in principle.

On BBC Television's *The Money Programme* just before the end of the year he defended Cavenham's success over the past decade with all the vigour he could muster. Indeed after the programme's first filmed report he had spent the next four days encouraging a team at Cavenham to prepare detailed responses to each and every criticism the programme raised. He then took the initiative once the live programme was on the air and did not allow his two interviewers, Hugh Stephenson, then editor of *The Times* Business News, and James Bellini of the BBC a chance to question him. He told them his version unaided.

He criticized the programme for not getting its facts right, for not allowing a proper representation of his company's achievements: and he demonstrated for more than half an hour that he was not prepared to sit back and be ignored. It was a performance that would so delight some businessmen that they would keep a videotape of it in their offices as proof that a businessman could turn against anyone who criticized his achievements, even though it convinced some viewers that his passion for his own achievements bordered on the compulsive. It certainly did not delight many journalists.

12. More than a Piece of Paper

From the outside the office block at the top of the Avenue de Friedland, a stone's throw from the Champs Elysées, looked ordinary enough. Six storeys of nineteenth-century respectability, solid to each of its grey stone walls, restrained behind its glass and iron doors, but still with the touch of marble in the hallways that marked its affluence. Inside the noise of the traffic pulling up before it turned into the swirl around the Place de L'Etoile was hardly more than a faint murmur.

Yet in the corridor of Générale Occidentale's offices on the fifth floor there was one discreet door among the light wood and soft grey carpets that led not only to a single stairway but also to an office which was quite out of the ordinary. There was the separate room for a secretary, a small boardroom, two sofas, a coffee table and a small antique desk, but one end of the room was panelled not in mahogany but glass. Beyond it was not a tiny balcony but a low-walled terrace with its own garden, the length of an English cricket pitch and as wide as the Royal Lawn at Ascot, complete with lawn, shrubs and flower beds. The garden looked straight out on to Napoleon's monument, the Arc de Triomphe, with not a single building to obstruct the view. Bonaparte himself would have approved. This office was now the heart of Jimmy Goldsmith's empire.

The *New York Times* had recently accused him of 'trying to freeze out the little investor': he owned more than 30 per cent of the group himself, whereas the other major shareholders, who each owned no more than 10 per cent, were principally large institutions in France who had been with him for some time, including the Union des Assurances, Renault and his merchant bankers Hambros, although in March 1979 the French Compagnie Générale d'Electricitie was also to take a stake. In the past year he had virtually completed his five-year plan for consolidating the companies and eliminating anything that was marginal to their main business, food; manufacturing it and retailing it. Now he was anxious to expand again, but he was also anxious to make sure of the future of Générale Occidentale.

Affairs in England had become more and more miserable. Cavenham may have been a success there but there seemed to be no acknowledgement of that. There was just the incessant sniping at his achievements and a persistent snooping into his own life. At least in Paris he could go out when he wanted to without being followed by photographers and without the suspicion that anyone he talked to might repeat what he said so that he would find himself written about in the press all over again. In France he understood what was happening, and he had come to know and like President Valery Giscard d'Estaing, since he had first met him in 1972.

Not every company had enjoyed his same success over the past few years, as he had recently come to know only too well. One company in particular had not had the happiest run of commercial success, the Patino Mining Company, which was still run by his former father-in-law, Antenor Patino, even though the old man was now seventy-nine. Their mine had been nationalized in Bolivia, and neither had one or two other experiments they had tried in Portugal. The company was still profitable but it was not quite the glittering success that the directors had hoped. Perhaps aware of that, Antenor Patino had even asked him privately to become chairman, but he had turned the offer down because he was determined not to run the company directly.

Instead he had agreed to become a director, aware that the wounds of nearly a quarter of a century before had finally been officially healed, no matter what emotional damage remained. Jimmy Goldsmith was still driven to greater and greater objectives, but the original motivation was almost too far in the past to sustain speculation about its genesis. He did not spend time considering it. There was the future of his own companies to attend to.

First there was the question of Generale Alimentaire to

First there was the question of Générale Alimentaire to be sorted out. Then there was the ownership of GO. He had decided to launch a company in Hong Kong and call it Générale Oriental. That would own slightly more than 30 per cent of GO, and in turn that Hong Kong company would be controlled by another company he intended to found in Panama, which would be called Lido SA. He would keep 40 per cent of Lido SA and would ensure that the shares could not be sold to a non-resident of France without express permission.

No one would be able to pry easily into his affairs in the future. By the time John Aspinall's new gaming club opened in London in June 1978 everything would be settled. Aspinall's club, which he had helped with loans and guarantees of almost £2 million from his Argyle company – in exchange for the right to become an equal partner with 50 per cent of the equity if he exercised an option before 1988 – was only a hobby, like owning the restaurant Laurent in Paris. Jimmy Goldsmith had decided he should be allowed to have one or two interests outside his business, providing that they were profitable hobbies. Besides he liked helping his friends. 'Aspers' might say that ten of his twenty close friends were animals – he had always had a thing about tigers, insisting they were wiser than men – but Jimmy Goldsmith knew he was one of the ten, and what is more one who could be counted on.

But it was America not gaming clubs that occupied most of Jimmy Goldsmith's thoughts. As Aspinall's opened he had launched a bid for another supermarket chain, Colonial Stores, which had its base in Atlanta, Georgia, with annual sales of more than $1 billion and 369 stores in the south-east United States. By August Colonial had accepted the offer, which had cost $133 million, and had made Jimmy Goldsmith the eighth biggest supermarket owner in America with 840 supermarkets from the Canadian border to Florida and the Gulf of Mexico. His Acapulco plan was still in operation.

In October he told the 26th Congress of International

Chambers of Commerce, held in the unlikely surroundings of Disneyworld in Florida, 'British industry has become a cripple and the British nation has been impoverished ... Great Britain is an example of a society which has purposely reduced the scope for entrepreneurship.' It was a message he was to repeat with even greater force to the British Institute of Directors in London within six months, but not one destined to ensure his popularity among British businessmen or politicians.

Nevertheless he still had ties in England. Ginette and he had divorced during the summer, as quietly as they had married seventeen years before. Manes was now nineteen and Alix nearly fifteen, while Isabel, although he continued to help support her, had long ago become independent. There was nothing he wanted to change about his relationship with Ginette or indeed with his children in Paris, but he was aware of his responsibilities to his new son and daughter. He had decided to marry Lady Annabel Birley.

Perhaps Jimmy Goldsmith's attachment to Annabel was no longer in its first flush of youthful passion but he still enjoyed her company and their children. There had been other companions, as she knew, but he still liked to come back to their new house in Richmond to see them, just as he liked to see Ginette in Paris. It might not be the 'conventional' life but it suited him very well and he made no secret of it. All his friends knew exactly what he thought. He was not, he told one, 'about to be a humbug.'

Another person who knew he was not about to be a humbug was a young *Paris Match* reporter, Laura Boulay de la Meurthe, whom he had met that summer, and whom he had begun to see more regularly in New York where he had an apartment in the Carlyle Hotel. Annabel would visit New York from time to time, either to go shopping or bringing the children on their way back from a holiday in the Caribbean, but that did not present any difficulty. He had explained to her many times what he thought, and she knew what he was like.

Nevertheless he had decided to marry and to do so in Paris away from the prying eyes of the British press. So, late in October 1978, Jimmy Goldsmith began arranging the marriage, to take place in the middle of November. Annabel would fly to Paris the night before under an assumed name, and she would stay at the Ritz. He would not even tell her where the ceremony would take place. He would just collect her, and take her off to get married.

Even though it was no longer in Sir Max Aitken's hands, the *Daily Express* was once again to prove the tormentor of his plans. The paper's gossip column, William Hickey, had revealed his intention to marry two weeks before it happened, and – even worse – a reporter and photographer were then dispatched to Paris to describe the event for the *Express* readers. He was furious.

The *Express* reporter travelled to Paris on the same aeroplane as 'Mrs Vane' (as Lady Annabel had called herself for the flight) and had introduced himself to her. Indeed he even sent two dozen roses to the Ritz. At a loss to know what to do for the best, Annabel decided to keep quiet about the young man. She had enough on her mind without worrying about William Hickey's reporter. However, no sooner had she met her future husband than an *Express* photographer, Bill Lovelace, appeared out of the blue to take their photograph, and Jimmy Goldsmith lost his temper. He pulled the photographer into the doorway of his office building with the help of one of his staff, and wrenched the film out of his camera. In the scuffle the photographer had his camera and glasses broken, his knuckles skinned and his ribs bruised. It was the most bizarre wedding morning Annabel Birley could have imagined.

The ceremony was hardly over when her new husband began dictating a letter to *The Times* in London in protest. 'When a middle-aged couple who have shared their lives for fourteen years are able to marry it is appropriate that they should choose to do so with the dignity of silence,' he wrote. 'That is still possible in Paris ... However I would be ungrateful if I were to finish this letter without thanking the *Daily Express* for a wonderful wedding present – the legal opportunity to 'manhandle' a representative of its gossip column.' He maintained he had submitted the paper's fifty-one-year-old photographer to a 'citizen's arrest' under the French laws of privacy. It was an explanation that convinced neither the *Daily Express* nor the rest of Fleet Street. Once again he was described as a man given to absurd rages, uncontrolled passions and an obsession with secrecy. What was he trying to hide?

As the William Hickey reporter Christopher Wilson wrote in his reply in *The Times*, 'It seems extraordinary that a man of Sir James's position should then admit to being pleased to engage himself in a public brawl on his wedding day.'

Jimmy Goldsmith was unrepentant. For its part, the *Daily Express* seemed equally determined to continue reporting his activities. Soon it was announcing that its quarry was on holiday in Gstaad with his second wife only a matter of weeks after his third marriage. The fact that he had always spent the period between Christmas and the New Year with Ginette was of no consequence to them; it was behaviour they believed was sufficiently unusual as to be worth reporting.

But he had a surprise for his tormentors in Fleet Street; he had decided to launch an English equivalent of *L'Express*, a British weekly news magazine that would reflect what he believed the standards of journalism should be. He had considered the idea before, indeed he had even talked in the past about launching an intellectual monthly on the lines of *Encounter* as well, but now he was intent on putting the plan into action. He had already asked a small management team to look into the prospects while he searched for an editor. It was a decision which broke the rules he had so carefully constructed at Cavenham, where he had always left most appointments to others: but this was his own personal interest. The company's money might be being used but he alone was keen to see it off the ground.

Before the end of December 1978 Jimmy Goldsmith had found himself an editor. He had remembered that when Rupert Murdoch had sold him his *Express* A shares, Murdoch had intended to appoint the then assistant editor and political columnist of the *Sun*, Tony Shrimsley, as editor of the *Observer*, although he had also intended to appoint an editor-in-chief as well. Perhaps Shrimsley, whom he had never met, might make a good editor, but he would have to find out. By the end of the year it had been settled: Tony Shrimsley would indeed become editor of the new magazine; and Jimmy Goldsmith had also decided to talk to Patrick Hubter, the city editor of the *Sunday Telegraph*, whom he had known for some time. Hutber had always seemed to have a suitably sceptical view of journalists and journalism. Jimmy Goldsmith's aim was to choose the very best people for his new magazine.

He encountered two unexpected difficulties, however. First, there were some journalists who simply would not countenance working for him after his battle with *Private Eye*. Secondly, many journalists knew that past attempts to launch a weekly news magazine had failed. They knew that the firmly established British newspapers, with their regular daily sale, which were complimented by an equally strong collection of national Sunday newspapers often with free colour magazines were bound to make the task of launching any weekly magazine which its readers were expected to buy over the bookstall counter vastly speculative. The very best journalists he wanted to recruit were not always as optimistic as he was, if, that is, they were even prepared to consider working for him.

Jimmy Goldsmith was launching out into an industry of which he had no experience, and which he did not entirely understand: and every move he made would be examined in public and with considerable scepticism. No one within Cavenham had any real experience of publishing. As managing director of his new company, Cavenham Communications Limited, he had chosen Tony Fathers who had been responsible for the successful dietary breads, Slimcea and Procea, before they had been sold off in 1975, and who had since worked both for Bovril and on a marketing project for French cheese. It was not the obvious experience for a man who was now to be in overall charge of a magazine which was designed to break new ground in British journalism by making extensive use of colour photographs and printed much more quickly than the more familiar colour magazines with the Sunday newspapers.

When Fathers himself had expressed a certain surprise at his appointment he was told that he would have the advantage of being able to look at the problems of the industry with a fresh eye. It was an argument, certainly, but it was not a particularly convincing one given the complicated problems of newspapers and magazines, and it was even less convincing when Jimmy Goldsmith put beside his new managing director, an editor-in-chief who had never been directly responsible for a national newspaper or magazine in his career.

When he began to tell one or two of his friends that he would be taking a close interest in the project personally, there were those who began to wonder if his own confidence in his abilities to conquer any commercial field would stand up to this new, and complicated, challenge. But Goldsmith was undeterred. Besides, there were some who reassured him that there was no reason why his news magazine should not succeed. What failures there had been in the past had never had the benefit of his substantial financial resources.

In the first weeks of 1979, however, while his team of British journalists was being recruited, his plans for America took a new turn. It had been simply a question of finding the right company; he had not forgotten his original conviction that the staples of life had often provided him with the best investment in the past and in the middle of 1978 he had come across the old Diamond Match Corporation of New York, which had begun making safety matches, in 1882. Now renamed Diamond International, it was a conglomerate which packaged and retailed timber and which happened incidentally to produce more than half America's playing cards as well as paper plates for fast-food chains. With more than $1200 million-worth of sales, it was one of the 250 largest companies in the United States.

But Diamond had another advantage for Goldsmith: hidden among its assets of do-it-yourself shops and the rest were 1,600,000 acres of timber in the north-eastern United States. The old idea of an ecologically sound asset, for so long his brother's hobby horse, had remained in his mind. Unknown to almost anyone, for the past six months he had taken a considerable interest in Diamond International, codenaming the company 'New New World'. Then in January 1979 that interest reached the notice of Diamond's unsuspecting American stockholders: he announced that his American subsidiary had bought 4 per cent of the company's stock for $15 million. The company gave a sharp intake of breath.

There was another ecologically sound company in America, however, in which he was also about to show an interest, Basic Resources International, which was considering the possibility of searching for oil in the central American state of Guatemala – a project that Jimmy Goldsmith found very attractive. The British invasion of United States industry which had begun in the early 1970s, not long before he had bought Grand Union, and progressed as British American Tobacco had bought the Gimbels and Saks stores in New York and Sir Charles Forte's Trust House Forte had bought the Travelodge motel chain, was continuing apace.

Certainly the *New York Times* was prepared to admit by February that his takeover of Grand Union 'appeared to have matured successfully', even if it had suffered from 'severe growing pains' on the way. The man who had told *Time* magazine seven years before that he had learnt his management technique from 'the mistakes of US multinationals' was now clearly intent on showing them their own mistakes.

But by the end of January Goldsmith was back in England keen to get his news magazine off the ground. The first members of the editorial staff were being hired by his editor, and he was determined that they should be the best his money could buy. There had been attempts to start a news magazine in Britain before, but none of them had been properly financed. This time with £7 million in the bank, the editor would have enough money to hire whom he wanted and to offer them salaries then higher than was customary in Fleet Street. *Private Eye* decried the move as a thinly disguised form of bribery to persuade the uncertain to join what it called Goldsmith's 'Marmite' Train, but he was determined to show that he would not be shut out of the British press by a conspiracy of suspicion mounted by those sympathetic to *Private Eye*. In any case he felt strongly that he had a responsibility to provide a platform for his and others' views about the present state of Britain. As he told *Marketing Week* magazine, 'There is no virtue in silence or tolerance while one's community is being destroyed.'

It was a theme to which he returned at the Institute of Directors annual meeting at the Royal Albert Hall in March 1979. 'Today in Britain the average man is no longer able to choose his child's school, his doctor or his hospital,' he said, and went on, 'Bullying minorities have the right by law to set up flying squads to blockade our industry, our schools, our communities, and even to force the sick out of their hospital beds.' To a country which had just experienced a winter of strikes, including stoppages by its hospital workers and its local council manual workers, and was less than three weeks from its first General Election for five years, the sentiment stuck a chord. The biggest selling daily newspaper, the *Sun*, put it loudly on its front page, and the right-wing Freedom Association took double-page advertisements in other newspapers to repeat it.

His reputation as a man of extreme right-wing views was now firmly established in the received opinion of almost every journalist in Britain. In fact, his views had not always been accurately reported. One error that was particularly common after his speech at the Albert Hall was that he was in favour of some kind of corporate government, which would mean that businessmen rather than politicians would be reasonable for running Britain. In fact his argument was that 'it seemed absurd, when government was running 40 per cent of the nation's activities, that all its members should be chosen from among a couple of hundred MPs and not from the nation as a whole, as was the case in America', as he put it later.

Indeed in his speech to the Annual Conference of Editors and Publishers held by United Press International in October 1975 he had also described the likely outcome of arguments within the Labour Party, and in particular that the Labour Party was 'being hi-jacked to the left'.

'At the time,' he said later, 'my friends in the Labour Party called me paranoid. They are now all saying the same thing, but rather too late I am afraid. One is always suspected of paranoia when one sees things that other people do not see.'

Jimmy Goldsmith had proved he had a voice in the public debate, and was intent on ensuring that his new magazine kept not only his place but also others'. There would be those who disagreed; let them: he had always kept two left-wing columnists on *L'Express* alongside two right-wing ones. The suspicion that had surrounded him since the battle against *Private Eye* had begun was, however, making the task of appointing journalists to his new British magazine difficult. A string of distinguished reporters, correspondents and columnists began to turn down very substantial offers to work for him. Some told him privately that they did not believe the idea of a news magazine could succeed in Britain, others expressed private doubts about the qualities of the editor he had chosen while a few refused to have anything to do with him whatsoever. The fact that he had managed to attract both Raymond Aron from *Le Figaro* and the left-wing writer Olivier Todd to influential editorial positions on *L'Express* seemed to have no effect. The refusals mystified him.

Nevertheless some people had agreed to join. Patrick Hutber had accepted a directorship, and agreed to edit the city coverage, and Tony Shrimsley had appointed as a political columnist the *Daily Telegraph*'s parliamentary sketch writer Frank Johnson, multiplying his salary by two and a half in the process. But Shrimsley's efforts to reflect *L'Express*'s tradition of having both left-wing and right-wing columnists was meeting far less success. A series of possible columnists turned down his offers of salaries up to £25,000 a year, including the *Guardian*'s Peter Jenkins and Ian Aitken and the *Observer*'s Alan Watkins and Adam Raphael. It was becoming clear that the old wounds of the *Private Eye* battle were a great deal deeper than he had imagined. No matter what his intentions, and the assertion by his editor that his magazine was to have its own freedom of expression, some British journalists remained wary of him; others felt cautious about his choice of editor.

Jimmy Goldsmith remained undeterred. He had always believed in allowing the people he had chosen the right to make their decisions, and to get on with it. True, he had fired the editor of *L'Express*, Phillippe Grumbach, a year ago, after he had mounted what Goldsmith believed was too personal an attack on François Mitterrand (a French court eventually awarded Grumbach $500,000 in back pay and indemnities for the dismissal) but that was exceptional, he maintained. He normally allowed those who worked for him to go their own way. He might have the public reputation of the perpetual interferer, but as so often the reality was rather different from the public appearance. He believed the proprietor of a magazine or a newspaper was responsible for what went into it, and he never intended to ignore that conviction, but that did not mean he took every decision himself. Tony Shrimsley and Tony Fathers were left to make their own mistakes, even though he would send them confidential memos every week of his views about the magazine.

In the meantime he would devote himself to the question of the standards of journalists and fight the remnants of the old battle against *Private Eye*. So in June 1979, two years after he had settled the case, Goldsmith was in court over the magazine again, although this time as the defendant, rather than the plaintiff. One of *Private Eye*'s contributors, Michael Gillard, had sued him for damages for slander and libel over Goldsmith's accusation that he had blackmailed John Addey and on 10 June the case came before Mr Justice Neill in the High Court in London. For the second time Lady Annabel accompanied him to court, although this time she came as his wife.

Michael Gillard claimed that Goldsmith's 'terrible, wicked and very damaging' allegations of blackmail had meant that he had lived under a 'black cloud' for three years, and that they could gravely affect his employment as a journalist. But throughout the case Goldsmith steadfastly refused to retract one word. Instead, he defended his allegations on the grounds that they were true.

In the words of one reporter who sat through the five-day hearing, it was 'one of the most remarkable performances in a courtroom I have even seen', for although Goldsmith was the defendant in the case, he was not the person who, he claimed, had been blackmailed, that was John Addey, who was never even called as a witness.

After hearing Jimmy Goldsmith give evidence for more than a day, the jury decided that he had neither slandered nor libelled Michael Gillard.

For Jimmy Goldsmith it was a justification of his action against *Private Eye*, and one that he had waited a very long time to see. It was also an opportunity to return to his campaign. No sooner had the case been completed and he had been cleared of calling Michael Gillard a blackmailer than Goldsmith went on to the offensive. He not only attacked the British Press Council, the body responsible for upholding the standards of British journalism, for being 'unwilling to address itself to fundamental problems concerning the good health of our nation's press', but he also wrote to Vere Harmsworth, who had recently inherited his father's title of Lord Rothermere, complaining about his old adversary Nigel Dempster. Not long afterwards, Rothermere, as the chairman of Associated Newspapers, wrote to Dempster suggesting that his column in the *Daily Mail* was 'beginning to have the taste of old cold fried potatoes'. The enmity between Goldsmith and a number of British journalists had, if anything, become more acute. Even the satisfaction of winning his case against Gillard had not ended his savage feelings about them, and although some criticized his action against Dempster for being no more than belligerent bullying, with its flavour of 'tycoon talking to tycoon', he was simply convinced that the constant repetition of their views was preventing the dissemination of an accurate picture of Britain, and he was as determined as he had always been to stop it.

To most British journalists the possibility of a conspiracy in their eccentric trade, with its invincibly individualist traditions, seemed impossible. Ironically, while organized conspiracies might be possible among members of the far left, to most conventionally neutral British journalists Goldsmith's campaign against *Private Eye* and some individuals, like Dempster, seemed to be little more than further evidence of his extraordinary obsession. To Goldsmith, however, the consistency of the opposition he encountered in the press convinced him there was a conspiracy.

The atmosphere of accusation and counter-accusation, of mutual mistrust and suspicion had not been dispelled; and it hardly aided the foundation or the recruitment for his weekly magazine, which he had decided should be called *Now!* A list of 300 or so potential titles had been drawn up but there had been only two choices in his mind. It was either to be called 'Now!' or 'Today'. He chose *Now!*, complete with exclamation mark.

It was not the most auspicious background in which to launch any uncertain venture in British publishing let alone a news magazine. The bitterness of the past three and a half years had spread to every section of British journalism. Almost every journalist who agreed to work on *Now!* was deeply criticized for doing so by many of his former colleagues. So strong were the feelings that the magazine's new art director, Jeanette Collins, even had a glass of wine thrown at her by a former colleague from *The Times.* For whether he liked it or not, Jimmy Goldsmith had become a symbol to some journalists: they saw him as a rich bully, a man who was at worst malevolent and who thought his wealth and power gave him a licence to hush all criticism or opposition, however puny. To them he had become a threat to the freedom of the press and they did not believe *Now!* would change that. Yet for his part Jimmy Goldsmith took each and every one of their criticisms as further evidence of the conspiracy he believed there was against him. The atmosphere of distrust and suspicion had become so dank that every action of either side served only to fuel the other's prophecies.

Even more significantly for his future as a publisher in Britain, that atmosphere had also soured the attitude of advertisers to his magazine. Helped by a steady campaign in *Private Eye*, *Now!* failed to convince the advertising agencies that they should persuade their clients to buy advertisements in it. Goldsmith's reputation, and the suspicion that he had created among what he later called the 'trendies' in London advertising agencies made the already hazardous path of launching a new magazine in an uncertain economic climate considerably more treacherous.

By the middle of August 1979, only four weeks before *Now!* was due to appear on British bookstalls, Jimmy Goldsmith had become concerned at his editor's failure to lure enough senior editorial members of sufficient weight and authority. He believed one or two extra might be essential, and in August Jimmy Goldsmith approached the *Sunday Telegraph*'s distinguished columnist Peregrine Worsthorne with the suggestion that he might join, bringing with him another senior editor. He made the approach without consulting his editor, who, when he heard, resisted strongly. Worsthorne and Shrimsley met to discuss Worsthorne's role but they couldn't agree. Shrimsley dug his heels in. Goldsmith backed down and the negotiations with Worsthorne failed.

On Thursday, 13 September 1979, the first issue of *Now!* was launched at a grand breakfast in London amid a welter of publicity – it was even an item on the day's radio and television news broadcasts – and the 400,000 copies of the first issue sold out. Goldsmith hoped that perhaps he had been right to leave things alone. It was a hope that was not destined to be fulfilled.

Madame Beaux and others had been warning him that he must not allow his obsession with English journalism to obscure the importance of the developments he had set in train in America. There was still a great deal to be done, and a great many opportunities to be exploited. The explorations for oil near the Guatemalan border with Mexico were not proving as simple a task as Basic Resources had thought it might be – Major General Fernando Lucas Garcia's Government was demanding a greater control of their own resources in spite of an agreement they had signed; while some directors of the Diamond International Corporation were not pleased to find that a little over 4·2 per cent of their stock was now in the hands of a businessman with a reputation for fast takeovers.

The American supermarkets were doing well, as indeed was Bovril, but his plans for the future had to be attended to: publishing in Britain or France would have to take second place.

By the end of 1979 he had decided not to take up residence in the office which he had asked to be specially prepared for him at *Now!* This notion to move there, born in the optimistic days of the summer, had been gently discarded as the launch had taken place and the doubts about the quality of the team and product had slowly begun to grow, and as the demands of his other businesses reasserted themselves. In the nineteen months of the magazine's existence he would never occupy his office, just as he would never attend the magazine's weekly editorial conferences. For despite his public image as a man anxious to manipulate journalists, he remained studiously remote from them. He did not fire a barrage of memoranda of praise or condemnation as Lord Beaverbrook had done. Nor did his behaviour resemble that of the first Lord Northcliffe who besieged his journalists with telephone calls and strange requests. He contented himself instead with sending a confidential weekly memorandum to Tony Shrimsley detailing his views on the magazine. He seldom demanded that they be acted on, no matter how enthusiastically or not they had been received.

He had less and less time or inclination to take an active interest in *Now!*, which was not proving the success he had hoped. Nor had his enterprise in Guatemala, where he was to spend some months during the winter of 1979 and the spring of 1980, turned out to be an unqualified triumph. Madame Beaux had been drafted in and Basic Resources had begun to look for a partner in the enterprise, to share the burden of costs. Eventually they had found one in the French national oil company, Société Nationale Elf-Acquitaine. In November 1979 he bought the Texas chain of 100 J. Weingarten stores and the following month acquired the Caters chain from Debenham's in England. Publishing might be a risky venture, and so might oil, but supermarkets were much safer.

Owning supermarkets had become so much the predominant part of Jimmy Goldsmith's business that by the end of March 1980 it was becoming clear that he did not intend to remain a food manufacturer much longer. Selling groceries accounted for 93 per cent of his business and nearly 80 per cent of his trading profit, while manufacturing food accounted for less than 7 per cent of his business, 1 per cent of his profit. 'We are,' he told the London *Daily Mail*, 'the third largest food retailer in the world after Safeways and Kroger with sales of £3,000 million a year.'

Within a few weeks he and his fellow directors had come to the conclusion that 'Cavenham had reached the moment when it had to decide whether to concentrate its resources on manufacturing or retailing.' As he put it in the company's annual report, 'In view of the results achieved, the decision to concentrate on retailing was obvious.'

Hardly was the decision made than he had sold Bovril to the giant Beecham group for £42 million in cash; and Générale Occidentale had sold its food manufacturing interests to BSN Gervais-Danone in France. Within six months every remnant of what had once been a massive European food manufacturing group, the largest in Europe after Unilever and Nestle, had been dismantled. Felix had been sold in Sweden and Austria. The soft drinks makers T. W. Beach in England had been sold. Générale Alimentaire had been sold, as had other major interests in Sweden, Austria, Spain, Belgium and Holland. It was the most rapid dismemberment of an enterprise seen in Europe since the war.

As if to signpost the change, he then used part of the money raised by the sales to launch even further into Diamond International in America. Although Diamond's president, William J. Koslo, had said Goldsmith wanted 'control' at the 'lowest possible price' and he had made them a 'grossly inadequate offer', by the end of June Cavenham's American subsidiary owned 24 per cent of the vast group with its annual $55 million profits. The holding brought Jimmy Goldsmith a seat on the Corporation's board of directors.

It was one of the few boards of which he was to remain a member. In July 1980, three years after he had said that he no longer wanted to be the chairman of a public company, he resigned as chairman of Cavenham, to be replaced by Martin Plowden Roberts. In the words of his last annual report, 'As I am domiciled in France, it is wisest that I should concentrate my efforts on my job as chairman of Générale Occidentale ... As Générale Occidentale is Cavenham's ultimate holding company, I am happy that my association with Cavenham will continue.' On 19 August 1980 he had taken the £2·1 million already lost on *Now!* in England with him to Générale Occidentale. Cavenham would not be forced to bear the debt.

It was the first clear sign that the final withdrawal of Jimmy Goldsmith was under way, even though few people recognized it. For most people in England he remained, in the words of one journalist in *Punch* magazine, 'as recognizable as Robert Redford'. He did not enjoy it, and he intended to stop. He had already made up his mind.

13. *Now!* Becomes Then

No one, not even Lady Annabel Goldsmith herself, had really been expecting another child. After all she was forty-five, and the mother of two families. Rupert, Robin and Jane Birley were no longer children, but Jemima and Zacharias still occupied the nursery at Ormeley Lodge and she had even spent the past three years looking after her stepson Manes.

'I hadn't any intention of having any more children,' she was to say later, 'but Benjamin just popped out.' Although she had been seeing less of her husband over the past year and a half as the demands of the Guatemala exploration and the supermarket chain in America grew, she still enjoyed creating a new family for him; and for herself. In the past four years she had also had three miscarriages. 'I couldn't have gone off with a man who wasn't generous in spirit and loved his children,' she told her friends when they mentioned she seemed to have spent even more time alone since she had married Jimmy Goldsmith on that bizarre November day in Paris than she had done before. Wasn't she thinking of moving to America? But Annabel made it clear that she had no intention of abandoning the country of her birth and of her home.

'I'm English and the children are English,' she told anyone who asked. 'I would rather bring them up here, even if we don't see as much of Jimmy as we might do.' Some found her decision hard to understand, but they had forgotten that the Londonderrys were every bit as determined a family as the Goldsmiths, and the daughter of the 8th Marquis of Londonderry had been under remarkably few illusions about her relationship with her new husband for many years.

So as Benjamin Goldsmith moved into the nursery at Ormeley Lodge a few days after his birth on 28 October 1980 his father was not destined to become a familiar figure in the ritual of his daily life. But Jimmy Goldsmith was more preoccupied with the birth of his ambitions to take over the entire Diamond Corporation of America than the process of rocking his sixth child and third son off to sleep or seeing he was properly fed. But although he and Annabel had chosen his name aware that it implied there would be no more children, Jimmy Goldsmith cared a great deal for his new son, and for all his new family; he simply believed in living his life in compartments.

It was England that had come to depress him. His hopes for the country had evaporated, just as his hopes for political influence here had disappeared. He had, however, been able to persuade Prime Minister Margaret Thatcher to be the guest of honour at *Now!*'s first anniversary dinner on 14 September 1980. He had wanted to recreate some interest in the magazine, and the Prime Minister's after-dinner speech, which was televised live, clearly helped to do this. The whole occasion was such a success that he insisted on taking Annabel and Lady Falkender to celebrate afterwards at Aspinall's. But his opinion that England was no longer the place for him remained unaltered. It could be left to its own devices. There was no future for him.

Besides, the British press irritated him more and more. There seemed no chance he would ever be accepted as a successful businessman, instead he was always depicted as a man with two families, the demented pursuer of *Private Eye*, the scourge of journalists. Even though he had won the Gillard blackmail case, which he felt vindicated his campaign, and the Court of Appeal had not upheld an appeal against the decision, he was still always cast as the villain. And now *Private Eye* was taking its revenge. Their steady sniping at the claimed sales of *Now!*, which had provoked the magazine to issue a writ for libel in February, had clearly had its impact. The advertising agencies had begun to doubt *Now!*'s claims of a circulation of 125,000 a week. The magazine had initially boasted that it would reach a circulation of a quarter of a million; its achievement of half that number therefore seemed a failure, even though it was more than the combined sales of the *Listener*, the *New Statesman* and the *Spectator*. Once again his achievements, however small, seemed to be neglected in favour of sneers, and the thought depressed him.

Even more depressing, however, was *Now!*'s failure to establish a reputation for serious thought and analysis. It offered a respectable enough coverage of the week's news with photography, but it seemed to lack enough exclusive stories or the depth of coverage familiar in American news magazines. Glossy and with a large emphasis on colour photography, it seemed not quite authoritative enough. As his friends had begun to tell him more and more regularly, it had not become an indispensable part of either English intellectual or political life, even though he had free copies of the first issue delivered to MPs and senior civil servants to give it an opportunity to become so. Perhaps an editor with a different newspaper background might have had a clearer idea of the authority and weight he had hoped for, to bring *Now!* the reputation for serious thought and analysis he had wanted.

Soon after the New Year holiday in 1981 his worst fears for the magazine's standards seemed to be confirmed. It printed a rather breathless and not particularly considered account of President Giscard d'Estaing's chances in the forthcoming presidential elections, suggesting that the death of three cabinet ministers was somehow connected to the President and was therefore an important issue. The article infuriated him. It seemed to him to demonstrate one of the worst qualities of British journalism, the use of smear.

'The one thing I have always hated is personal attacks,' he said later. 'I believe in attacks on ideas not on personal grounds.' Incensed he demanded that the entire edition of the magazine be withdrawn and pulped. He did not want a single copy sold anywhere, he told Tony Fathers on the telephone; the cost did not matter. When Fathers told him he was too late to stop distribution in Britain, he ordered that no copies should be sent to France, or to the rest of Europe. 'It is everything I hate,' he said angrily.

It was another decision that provided ammunition for his critics. They used it as evidence that he was the interfering proprietor that they had always predicted he would be. 'I knew it would cause an argument,' he said later, 'but I took the stand on principle. It was perfectly obvious that banning the sale would create far more publicity than letting it go forward. So it was perfectly obvious that I would be doing harm to Giscard.' It may have been a principle to Jimmy Goldsmith but to many people in England it seemed the action of a man anxiously trying to protect the political reputation of his friends – including the President of France – and, by implication, an attempt to assure himself of political influence if not political power. Jimmy Goldsmith maintained that he did not mind attacks on Giscard – after all, *L'Express* had recently attacked the President's decision to meet President Brezhnev in Warsaw – but the quality and thought of *Now!*'s piece utterly depressed him. 'It was not a question of being for or against Giscard,' he said later, 'it was a question of being for or against the right standards of journalism in *Now!* and I objected violently to a cover of Mitterrand in *L'Express* which was not compatible with what I felt was decent journalism and this was despite the fact that I object profoundly to Mitterrand's policies.'

But if *Now!* was not living up to Jimmy Goldsmith's expectations, *L'Express* was surpassing them. The magazine in France was firmly established as the country's leading news magazine with a circulation of 550,000 copies each week. *Paris Match* was bigger still, but that relied more on pictures and less on words than did *L'Express*, whereas columnists and words had always been the cornerstone of *L'Express*'s success in Jimmy Goldsmith's eyes. He felt the staff was too large and sometimes acted arrogantly, but he did not intend to do anything about this at the moment.

By the end of March 1981 Goldsmith had seen almost all the food manufacturing interests of both Cavenham in Britain and Générale Occidentale in France sold. Cavenham's jams and preserves had gone to Chivers Hartley, the confectionary to Enterbrook Limited, and within a few months the liqueur chocolates were sold to four of their directors for £8 million and became the new Famous Names brand.

The original foundations of the company he had built seventeen years before had been quietly dismantled. In their place his empire now rested on three legs: super-markets in America and Britain (he had not sold the profitable Allied Suppliers chain of Presto and other super-markets); Basic Resources International, including the oil interests in Guatemala; and his holdings in Diamond International. Guatemala had not been quite the success he had hoped, but Madame Beaux had managed to extricate the copy from some of its difficulties with the Government, and had arranged their partnership with the French national oil company which had saved the experiment from catastrophe, but it had taught him a lesson. In future he would concentrate on countries whose traditions and way of working he understood. South America might be interesting to explore at some time in the future, but for the moment his energies had to be directed at North America where he knew the ground rules. That meant expanding his interests in Diamond International with all possible speed.

But as winter gave way to an unexpectedly mild spring in 1981 Jimmy Goldsmith was also thinking of making another fundamental change in his financial empire. He was seriously considering selling the Banque Occidentale, which Madame Beaux had so carefully nurtured during the past decade and which had helped the group during some of its most complicated financial dealngs. He had been beginning to wonder if it had not outlasted its usefulness, and whether instead they should be concentrating more of their efforts in America. Generale Occidentale would re-main his master company in France, but was the Banque really necessary any longer? He had already been ap-proached about its future by those who believed the social-ist François Mitterrand would win the presidential elections in May and immediately nationalize the banks still in private hands. But that possibility did not perturb him particularly. What was more important was how he could best use his closest associates. For throughout the life of his companies he had trusted very few people and he still believed in using those few people carefully – where he needed them most.

First, however, he had to decide what to do about *Now!*.

Madame Beaux had already told him it was occupying too much of his time, and, as he was to say to the American magazine *Newsweek* a few weeks later, she had also said, 'When a loss is no longer an investment but becomes a subsidy then it is time to close down.'

So when the projected budgets for revenue and expenditure were presented to him at the beginning of April he knew he had no choice, they made such dismal reading. There was no sign of *Now!* breaking even in the foreseeable future, and no clear sign that it would ever do so. There were just larger and larger losses to be born. There were loyal readers certainly, but not enough of them, nor were they powerful enough or affluent enough to encourage the advertising agencies to place sufficient advertisements. The time had come to admit defeat, and to do it quickly and as painlessly as possible. Jimmy Goldsmith decided that *Now!* would close before the end of the month. It was exactly four years since he had seemed on the brink of buying the London *Evening Standard*. April had turned out to be a cruel month for Jimmy Goldsmith's ambitions as a publisher in England.

Just before Easter he summoned Tony Fathers to Grand Union's offices in New York and broke the news to him. Together with another Cavenham director, Ian Duncan, Fathers then started to work out the mechanics of the closure. The magazine had already lost nearly £8 million, but Fathers and Duncan were not told to keep within a budget. The magazine was to be closed, but not scuppered. Everyone would be properly paid off.

Within twenty-four hours Fathers had taken Concorde back to London. But it was not until the following week that the news of the decision reached the editor of *Now!*, Tony Shrimsley. It was only then that Fathers delivered a letter to him from Jimmy Goldsmith suggesting that he come to Paris the following day to talk about the future of the magazine. The letter made it clear that they were going to be talking about closing down.

On Friday 24 April Jimmy Goldsmith paced up and down the grass of his terrace overlooking the Arc de Triomphe and explained to Shrimsley that the decision to close had been the hardest he had ever had to take, but there was no alternative. Everyone would be well treated but it could not go on. He did not say he had lost interest in it more than a year earlier when it had failed to live up to his own hopes, instead he just asked how they should announce the decision.

Shrimsley was so shocked that, as he said later, 'Almost the only thing I could think of was that the grass needed cutting,' – he even told an astonished Goldsmith during their conversation that it did. But finally they agreed that rather than meet the cost of another edition Shrimsley would announce the decision to close as Jimmy Goldsmith could not leave France until the Thursday. To make it seem there was no panic he would not tell his editorial staff until the following Monday morning even though several senior editors traditionally attended a Sunday morning conference. Shrimsley was anxious that things should seem to be quite normal. It was a loyal decision by Shrimsley to bear the brunt of the criticism of the closure, but a misguided one; it made Jimmy Goldsmith appear a man frightened to face the consequences of his own decisions, hiding from the fate of a magazine whose launch he had attended personally. Some of his staff also felt the closure itself broke a commitment on BBC television to sustain the magazine for at least four years. It was an absence few journalists would forget.

When the news of the closure was finally announced on Monday 27 April, all Goldsmith could tell the journalists who telephoned him in Paris was, 'I wanted it to succeed, but not so badly that I intoxicated myself to the facts when it did not.' With an audited circulation of 119,000 copies a week, he added, 'I look at it all with affection, and I regret losing my voice in the national debate of a country I care about. But I am no longer one of the players.' As he told *Newsweek*, 'We are just grocers now.'

Indeed he was. On the same morning that the closure of *Now!* was announced, Cavenham told the stock market that it would be applying to change its name back to Allied Suppliers (Holdings), the name of the largest of the companies it had taken over. The name of Goldsmith's grandfather's house in Suffolk would disappear from the English financial scene. It was to remain only as the name on Allied

Suppliers dull six-storied headquarters in the industrial waste land near London's Heathrow Airport. More than anything else it was a sign that as a businessman Jimmy Goldsmith was no longer interested in England.

What the *Observer* had called 'the boldest publishing launch since the war' had become one of the most public, and inexpensive, failures. With the loss of more than 120 jobs, including the redundancy of 80 journalists, the final loss would approach £10 million, or almost the equivalent of giving every reader a £1 note when he bought one of the eighty-four issues during the nineteen months of its life.

Jimmy Goldsmith made a point of coming to England at the end of the week in which *Now!*'s closure was announced. He had decided to come to the wake which the management had arranged to mark the magazine's demise; but he also asked his security adviser to keep a closer eye on him than usual. There had been threats of left-wing demonstrations after his apparent guarantee of work, in spite of his offer that 'Anyone with any specific difficulties should come to me directly'. In the basement of a warehouse he had once owned he saw the end of a magazine he had once had high hopes for. Like so many of his experiences with the British press, his hopes had turned to dust.

Perhaps his lack of a strategy for publishing had been against him, perhaps he had not known enough about it to convey to the editor what he had in mind, perhaps the British had come to suspect him too much ever to support any magazine or newspaper he owned, or perhaps it was simply that he did not depend on it for his income as Beaverbrook or Northcliffe had done. He had been a dabbler in the British press, not a magnate. For a man with Jimmy Goldsmith's pride it was a depressing conclusion.

Within a week it would seem that none of his ambitions in publishing would be without their difficulties, for just as *Now!* closed *L'Express* published a cover which depicted the two candidates for the French presidential elections. It showed François Mitterrand looking a great deal younger than his opponent Valery Giscard d'Estaing, even though he was in fact nearly ten years older. In the words of one left-wing daily paper in Paris, 'Jimmy Goldsmith saw red.'

Although, as the *Observer* in London had commented two years previously, 'Goldsmith believed that a left-wing government would have been a "catastrophe" for France', he had nevertheless allowed his deputy editor, the Cambridge University-educated former BBC television presenter Oliver Todd, to urge the magazine's readers 'to vote for the Socialist–Communist coalition'. He had also allowed another *L'Express* columnist, the French author Max Gallo, to do so as well. But he had never intended the magazine to become the voice of the socialist or communist party. Todd and Gallo's views were always 'balanced by two right-wing columnists', one of whom was the distinguished Professor Raymond Aron. But the principle that the magazine as a whole should remain independent of both government and opposition, and free to attack whichever government was in power, seemed to him essential if it were to retain its place as France's leading news magazine. But even beyond that, Goldsmith did not intend to own a magazine which supported an editorial line he believed was evil: he did not believe in interfering in editorial matters usually, but he would not hesitate to stop a magazine whose editorial line disturbed him, no matter what the success or profitability of the magazine might be.

So, less than a fortnight after *Now!* closed, he summoned Oliver Todd to the *L'Express* offices in Paris and fired him. Within a matter of hours the editor Jean François-Revel had also resigned, and a string of other editorial men had threatened to leave. But Jimmy Goldsmith was unmoved. The staff had one choice, he told them, 'either submit to my new role as editor-in-chief or resign'. He declared in his first editorial in his new role, '*L'Express* remains liberal', and it would be the 'strongest voice in opposition'. He was not to remain in direct control for long, only to oversee the charge at the top of the editorial team.

Two days after the departure of Todd and Revel he repeated his ultimatum, and in the most dramatic way, Jimmy Goldsmith launched an extraordinary attack on the staff. At a bitter meeting he told them all that the economic situation would not be strong enough in the future under the politics of the new Socialist government for him to go on supporting *L'Express* unless he had confidence in it, and the cover had made him lose that confidence.

He had come within an inch of closing the magazine down. When he was accused in turn of being interested only in supporting his friend Valery Giscard d'Estaing he called his critics the intellectual 'pus' at the heart of society. The air was thick with accusations and counter accusations and with his old suspicions of journalists, and he made it clear that he would only continue to support *L'Express* while it reflected his principles. If that were not possible then he would close it down.

But his well publicized rage, which captured the imagination of every other Paris newspaper, had another benefit for Jimmy Goldsmith. It gave him the chance to 'put an end to the prima donnas', as one *L'Express* man called some of the magazine's highly paid staff. His irritation over the cover also provided him with the opportunity he had been looking for to take action to put the magazine back on the footing he wanted it: to ensure there was a smaller staff more committed to his point of view and that it would therefore go on to make a substantial and continuing profit. As Tom Sebestyen, the managing director of *L'Express* and a friend since 1956, put it later, 'When the final straw alone breaks the camel's back then it seems surprising that a single straw should break it.'

By the end of the week in which he had assumed control sixty-two people had left the staff of *L'Express*, and Jimmy Goldsmith had not sold it. The battle had been brief and bitter, and it had confirmed the view of the new socialist government that he was their implacable opponent, but in his mind he had established *L'Express* as an independent voice again.

But even though it did not lie behind his actions either at *Now!* or *L'Express* Jimmy Goldsmith had reached another conclusion about journalists after his experiences during the previous four years. He had reached the conclusion some years before that they were as susceptible to being corrupted as any other profession, and he had become convinced they had been infiltrated by the communists. As he had told the Tory Party Media Committee of the British House of Commons at the beginning of the year, 'There are many hundreds of magazines and bulletins published by the front organizations. And there is the use of apparently objective media. This is achieved either by subsidizing them or by penetrating them with journalists who are sympathetic to Communist propaganda.'

To most people in Britain it seemed yet another example of his hysterical right-wing views, the outburst of a man who saw reds under every bed, and was intent on declaring it on every street corner. The circulation of his speech to the committee, with its allegations of infiltration of the German news magazine *Der Spiegel* by the Russian secret service seemed only to confirm that view. The accusation drew a massive writ for libel damages from *Der Spiegel*, when it was reprinted in *Now!*, a claim which he still intended to contest with all the vigour he had brought to his case against *Private Eye*, but it was a further sign that he had come to see himself in the role of Savonarola, a prophet bound to be martyred. Grotesque self-delusion or not, Jimmy Goldsmith had come to believe his views would always be ignored by the majority of intellectually respectable opinion in Britain; as he had said before, 'One is always suspected of paranoia when one sees things that others do not see.'

By now that could not have concerned him less. The man who had always been convinced that he was an outsider no longer aspired to be accepted by the intellectual establishment. 'I am the opposite of an intellectual in the French sense,' he was to say later. Indeed he had told the Harvard Business School Club days before he had closed *Now!*, 'The Liberal intellectuals are unable to distinguish tolerance from strength and tolerance from weakness.' He had no wish to be weak, and that was what he felt most intellectuals were: weak enough to accept infiltration.

The vehemence with which he expressed those views, which he repeated in an article in the *Guardian* in July 1981 – 'For years every strategic centre of British life has been infiltrated systematically by the far left. The purpose has been to undermine, destabilize, demoralize and when the conditions are ripe, to take over' – served only to alienate him still further from the conventional social and political tradition in Europe, and he rather enjoyed that. The middle class could see him as demented if they wanted to, as a mad right-wing extremist. He had his own answer, as he put it in the *Guardian*, 'Those who have attempted to alert public opinion have been ridiculed and described variously as extremists or cranks.'

Jimmy Goldsmith had come to see himself as a prophet doomed to be ignored, and it had helped him to explain the bitterness of the attacks on him, and the deliberate misunderstanding he received in the British press. He had not lost his conviction that British journalism needed to have its standards examined. He believed the public should be informed of 'the sources of finance of publications and of payments made to individual journalists'.

In a letter to *The Times* in September 1981, which had almost not been printed until Goldsmith threatened to put it in every other British newspaper as an advertisement under the heading 'The letter *The Times* refused to print', he argued, 'In Britain we hear a great deal about interference in editorial matters by proprietors of newspapers. Yet we hear almost nothing about the interference in editorial matters by foreign governments who have made payments to journalists.' He had no intention of letting his conviction be ignored. He announced in his letter the funding of 'an annual prize of £50,000 for the best investigative journalism into subversion in the media'.

The offer of such an enormous sum, fifty times more than the annual Journalist of the Year Award, and a hundred times more than the American Pulitzer Prize, attracted some scepticism, particularly from his old adversary the *Sunday Times*. The paper commented, 'If Sir James's prize does uncover manipulation by communist governments, the revelation will astonish in particular the authors of millions of words of research and analysis which have, over the years, tended to demonstrate not a bias to the left but exactly the opposite.' To most people who read it, and even to most journalists, however, his accusations seemed just another exaggerated outburst, another example of Jimmy Goldsmith's demented behaviour. They did not think for a moment that he might be right, any more than members of the British Labour Party several years before had been convinced by similar accusations about their organization. He was simply a right-wing businessman who probably did not have enough to occupy his mind. That, however, was not the case. There was a good deal on his mind besides the idea of infiltration in the British media.

By September 1981 he was finally ready to move to America and the final move was to sell the Banque Occidentale to his partners Credit Lyonnais, France's second largest bank (and already shareholders in Générale Occidentale). The sale meant that he even lost his office in the City of London in Leadenhall Street.

Allied Suppliers was now his only remaining holding in England, and even though he took an office in their Colnbrook headquarters he rarely went there, preferring instead to operate from Ormeley Lodge. In France Madame Beaux did not know precisely what the future held for her after she had finished the detailed negotiations of his withdrawal. She only knew he was intent on keeping just one or two interests in Europe, including *L'Express*, the Laurent restaurant on the Champs Elysée, and the potential half-share of Aspinall's Club in London. Nothing else remained apart from the 970 food stores run by Allied Suppliers which was to be given a budget of £145 million for new capital investments over the next five years to help ensure their success. But Madame Beaux knew that what he had in mind was the final march into the United States.

In October 1981 he had announced his stake in Diamond International was now 40 per cent, and only two months later he launched a full-scale bid for complete control of the hundred-year-old corporation that had pioneered the safety match. It was among the biggest takeovers launched in recent American history by a company controlled by a single individual, because he was prepared to pay over $400 million for the $700 million corporation. He was already 'the sixth largest overseas investor in the United States', as he told his friends proudly, and he had every intention of becoming the largest. With one of the biggest departures ever seen in Europe by a major company, the

Acapulco plan had finally come off. The only place where the name of Goldsmith's grandfather's house, Cavenham, now existed on one of his companies was in the United States.

14. As One Door Closes ...

The certainty and confidence were nothing new. At the age of six, when Jimmy Goldsmith was just beginning to enjoy life in the Caribbean, he told his anxious father that he did not need to learn to read. 'When I'm old enough I shall be a millionaire and have someone to read for me,' he said firmly.

Both his parents shook their heads. They knew they would never understand him. Indeed Madame Goldsmith, who still lives in Paris not far from where she and her husband spent much of their time, is still not sure that she understands her son, or his precociousness, even though they speak to each other several times a week in the family's patois. But the Goldsmith's are, as they have always been, a close family. In the difficult days both his mother and his brother Teddy helped the boy who was convinced he would be a millionaire with loans and guarantees. He has never forgotten it.

But the woman who helped him to create a financial empire with an annual turnover approaching $10 billion does understand it. Sitting in her office in the Avenue Friedland with its view of the Arc de Triomphe, but without Jimmy Goldsmith's Napoleonic terrace, Madame Gilbert Beaux looks more like a piano teacher than the woman who has regularly been called 'the best banker in France', and has been his partner since 1968. Her grey hair is pulled into a bun, and she is hardly tall. Her clothes are restrained as a teacher's, even if her blouse is silk. Perhaps the only sign of success is her gold eye make up.

'Jimmy wakes up every morning convinced that he has nothing at all,' she says with a piano teacher's firmness. 'Every morning we are rich only up to a point, the point at which the company has the ability to make growth and profits. All his money is tied up in the group and he is therefore only as good as the group's performance. If he is in the group he has to work, if he does not want to work he has to sell his participation, there can be no middle way.' She taps her desk with a pencil, like a baton.

'He has never been something in the middle, he is not a bourgeois. He does not put a little money here and a little money there. He prefers to believe he can continue to create for the group, and that is because he is both a peasant and the member of a great Jewish family.'

While his critics remain convinced that his aim is either political power, or at least political influence as a publisher, Madame Beaux persists quietly, 'He likes power naturally, but he also likes profits. They and the growth mean that he can indulge himself in the press or in other things. They bring him all of them.'

Since 1968, she has been the voice of moderation in Générale Occidentale and Cavenham; the hand of restraint on Jimmy Goldsmith's shoulder. It was Madame Beaux's influence, perhaps more than any other, that ended his action against *Private Eye* in England and suggested the demise of *Now!*, for while Jimmy Goldsmith is partly a liberal romantic, prone to grand gestures and sweeping opinions, Madame Beaux represents the sterner voice of reason he has always listened to.

'Most popular views of Jimmy Goldsmith are entirely wrong,' she says sternly. 'He is not a man of fixed views. He has the quality to change, to move, to adapt very quickly: and to abandon what he thought would be a strong point. He is far less of a gambler than we hear when it comes to business.' It is a Frenchwoman's appetite for deflating men and their myths.

'People cannot understand his success. So they say he has to be a gambler, because it has to be something they do not understand, and therefore something bad. No one is prepared to admit that we may have worked a little harder and thought a little more. I would not like to say we have taken no risks, that would not be true, but before Jimmy takes a risk he looks at it more than anyone can imagine.' It is a view which punctures a myth that even Goldsmith himself sometimes likes to perpetuate about himself – that he is prepared to sacrifice everything for one more throw on the red, one more turn of pitch and toss: the slightly thoughtless playboy who got lucky. It is a fantasy which he himself likes to sustain, for it makes him appear more foolish than he is. For beneath the six-year-old's *braggadocio* there is the shrewdness of a man who likes his opponents to underestimate him, to fail to see the pattern he is working to. This is the businessman who did not buy financial companies during the boom years of the 1960s as some did, anxious to make money quickly; instead, he bought the basics of the European pantry.

'People do not understand that business is both his hobby and his passion,' explains his former partner and close friend Selim Zilkha. 'He probably enjoys it almost more than anything else he does.' Certainly Jimmy Goldsmith is given to waking up in the middle of the night worried about what to do next, wondering how he can get what he wants, and sticks to a strategy much more carefully prepared than many suspect: but he also likes a fight.

Jim Slater, for example, believes he is 'like John McEnroe, he likes to feel the world is against him. It makes his adrenalin flow. He likes the fight to overcome them.' This may provide one explanation for his determination to conquer América, often against the wishes of the companies he had in mind to take over, when he could have remained peacefully and profitably in Europe. Neither Colonial Stores nor Diamond International were particularly keen to see the arrival of a businessman with such an international reputation for aggression in their boardrooms.

'There is no way I was ever going to tailor what I did to get a better reputation,' he maintains. 'Reputation is every bit as important as your leg, but I could not tailor what I was going to do to get a better press.'

Jimmy Goldsmith has a fanatic's disregard for prevailing opinion, whether it is right or wrong. He has always tended to see himself as a doomed prophet, whose achievements are usually belittled, and this has strengthened his tendency to cast himself as an outsider no matter which country he is in. 'I love America but I am a European,' he is fond of saying, 'and I am too English in France and too French in England.' Jim Slater believes 'he almost needs the feeling of being an outsider to survive.'

Perhaps that has led him to buy a 400,000-acre ranch

in the right-wing state of Paraguay. He does not intend to live on it, any more than he intended to live on the vast *hacienda* in Argentina which his company once owned. It simply represents an investment which he will defend, studiously ignoring the critics who describe the Paraguayan Government as repressive. It is not the reaction of someone anxious to create a political reputation.

Few of Jimmy Goldsmith's friends have ever believed he wanted a conventional political career. Some, like the British novelist and former Member of Parliament Jeffrey Archer, believe he may have wanted a seat in the House of Lords as a shortcut to the Cabinet, but most argue that he has never shown any tendency to alter his plans to meet what could be described as the demands of political expediency. 'I find it very difficult to believe that this is all he would have done if he had a very profound desire to be in politics,' is the conclusion of Tom Sebestyen of *L'Express*. The assumption is that if he had wanted it badly enough he would have ensured he got it.

Nevertheless among those who are not his friends the suspicion that the man whom his brother Teddy once said 'wanted to be Prime Minister or nothing' is a dictator in the making – intent on building a vast financial empire as a prelude to political domination – is not dispelled. Indeed at the age of forty-nine Jimmy Goldsmith knows he will probably never escape it, and as a result he has begun to accept that a traditional political career is unlikely to be open to him. 'My shame in politics is that I have never done anything,' he says now, aware that 'although I am a Reaganite and not on the far right' that is not how most people view him. It is no surprise that he counts former President Richard Nixon among his friends. The sense of rejection heightens his sense of being persecuted, to add to his determination to succeed in other ways, and by doing so to answer what he calls 'the biological necessity' of sustaining the Goldsmith name.

Jim Slater, whose opinions he still seeks about market movements, not only believes that Jimmy Goldsmith needs the sense of being an outsider to survive but also that he intends to become one of the world's truly 'super rich'. His brother Teddy suspects that the wounds of the attack on him as a young man by Antenor Patino have also fuelled that determination over the years. Neither man doubts that Jimmy Goldsmith is now intent on joining the select group of internationally wealthy men, whose lives become the subject of speculation and yet of increasing isolation.

Jimmy Goldsmith will surely not disappear entirely into the paranoid seclusion of a Howard Hughes, or the studied anonymity of Daniel K. Ludwig, but he seems more than ever determined to remove himself from the world of ordinary men. Like his brother Teddy, who has decided to sell his farm in Cornwall in favour of spending his time in Tuscany, Paris and at his new wife Kathy's home in New Zealand, Jimmy Goldsmith is on the brink of disappearing from European life. The homes and offices in Paris and London will remain, as indeed will his families in both cities. Who knows, he may even return, but for the present he seems determined to retire behind the walls that considerable wealth can bring. It is a trait which runs in the Goldsmith family.

When his uncle Baron Max Goldschmidt-Rothschild received the Gestapo at his home in Germany in 1939 he sent his butler to the door. The servant duly asked if they had an appointment to see the Baron, and on learning they did not, refused to let them see him. The Gestapo, so the family legend runs, never returned to bother the banker.

Certainly the last four years of attacks and criticism, of bomb threats to his solicitor's offices during the *Private Eye* case, and hints of kidnapping (at one stage a security device was installed in his office lavatory) have taken their toll. There was even a series of anonymous threats to kidnap two of his and Annabel's children in 1980, and those closest to him have noticed that his original preoccupation with secrecy has grown into an obsession. He now fears attack on himself or his family, although he also insists he 'is prepared to die' for what he believes in. Yet again it is not the response of a man given to moderation.

He will not be fifty until 1983, but he looks older. In spite of the perpetual tan that only the affluent seem able to sustain, the pouches under his eyes are deeper than they were. He has lost none of his liking for a fight, however. 'If anyone thinks he would not take on *Private Eye* again they are wrong,' Jim Slater maintains. 'He still relishes the idea of a fight if it is about something he believes in.' Indeed he also says, 'I realize that I had to withdraw if I was going to continue the fight against those who want to destabilize society.'

Not that Jimmy Goldsmith spends all that much time fighting anyone. His circle of friends is both small and close. Apart from his family, his three closest friends, Digby Neave, John Aspinall and Selim Zilkha, stretch back at least twenty years. There is then a second less intimate group including David Frost, Jim Slater and financier Gordon White. But altogether he and his circle are largely cocooned against the pressures familiar to most daily lives, and this can breed therefore sometimes rather humid and overwrought opinions, while it also reinforces his remoteness.

So although his ability to become temporarily absorbed in the details of one of his interests will remain – as it has always done – there seems a danger that Jimmy Goldsmith will spend more and more of his time shuffling his financial interests like a backgammon player, more preoccupied with the abstruse pleasures of the international financial world than the creation of another empire with its roots firmly in the everyday world.

'Jimmy is now in a position to do exactly what he wants to,' Madame Beaux explains. 'He can do anything he chooses. But he needs to have roots and to participate in communities. That is why he has always had industrial or retailing companies. He needs to have this kind of apprehension of life.'

The temptation for him to retire to the highest peaks of the financial world, like some doomed prehistoric monster which descends only when there is something it wishes to capture seems increasingly great. His enemies will seldom glimpse him (although they have rarely bothered to meet him), while his friends will remain as protective of him as they have always done: afraid as much for his vulnerability as of his strength.

Jimmy Goldsmith once said, 'The secret is to create new ambitions the whole time.' It was a remark worthy of the man whom perhaps he is most in danger of coming to resemble, Charles Foster Kane. It has yet to be seen whether he will try to create his own Xanadu.

Epilogue

For the moment, however, Jimmy Goldsmith's story ends where it began, in a hotel suite; although now there is the distant thunder of Madison Avenue beneath his window rather than the gentler hubbub of the Boulevard des Capucines. The Brooklyn iceman has replaced the baker from Montmartre.

The Carlyle is not one of New York's more ostentatious hotels, it is both discreet and restrained. From his suite there, which was specially decorated for him in the most modern style with Lady Annabel Goldsmith's help, he can look across Manhattan to the trees around the Metropolitan Museum on the edge of Central Park, a block to the West. Although he cannot quite make out the cages of the Park's Zoo (they are too far to the south) if he could, he might recognize his affinity to one of New York's most famous inhabitants, its polar bear. For he and the bear are both characters of weird and forceful originality, thought sadly neurotic by some and genuinely imaginative by others.

Jimmy Goldsmith certainly tends to pace up and down his suite as restlessly as a man who is himself in a cage, watching whoever is talking to him with his clear china-blue eyes as if he is a little afraid the watcher may strike him, although at his most frightened he can also be at his most dangerous. It gives him the impression of someone who wishes to remain a moving target. But unlike the bear he spends a great deal of his time on the telephone and chain-smoking Davidoff Number One Havana cigars.

But the Carlyle Hotel is not really his home, in spite of the fact that he now spends more time than he does anywhere else in the world. For Jimmy Goldsmith is still a nomad, a man who is not truly at home anywhere. 'I am both French and English,' he says quickly, tearing two chewed inches from the bottom of his cigar. 'Both a Jew and a Catholic, both a peasant and an aristocrat.' The implication is that he belongs nowhere, and that contradiction lies at the heart of his character.

He is both 'gentleman and adventurer, self-made man and cousin of the Rothschilds, a liberal and a man of the extreme right, a man of pleasure and a man of principle' as the left-wing Paris newspaper *Liberation* once put it. But he is also both a man who likes to be noticed, but who has come to detest the flame of publicity he was once attracted to; a man who loves his children but who can sometimes not see them for weeks at a time; a man who likes to be married but has the attitude of a bachelor.

The contradictions make him an exaggerated figure, prone to such manifest excesses that he convinces more conventional men that he is possessed of a dangerous degree of arrogance and self-delusion. It tends to confirm the impression of his critics that his success has somehow been accomplished only by sleight of hand, or with the dexterity of a mountebank who bewilders others by the speed of what he does. For them he is a juggler whose hands move too fast to be trusted, and who steadfastly refuses to tread the familiar paths of the modern world.

Undeniably there is a medieval quality about him. He behaves more like a mongol chieftain than a twentieth-century businessman, not only pitching his own tent wherever he intends to conquer, but also ushering his tribe of family and friends around the world, providing them with food and shelter and fighting on their behalf. One of them once described him as 'Attila the Hun with financial genius' and it was not an insult. It is as if he were a man born out of his time.

Even his superstitions are medieval. Jimmy Goldsmith tends to touch wood when he mentions something that he wants to happen; he dislikes describing any transaction he is involved in while it is still taking place in case it brings bad luck, and he is convinced that some people and places bring him good luck just as he believes other things can bring him bad. He is especially superstitious about the bad luck rubber bands – indeed almost anything made of rubber – can bring.

His political opinions, too, have a strain of thirteenth- and fourteenth-century Persia about them. Just as he despises the far left, so too he sees the British Conservative Party 'sickened by its own weakness, dominated by an old ruling class whose day is gone'. It is the analysis of a Genghis Khan, not a conventional Conservative, and a conclusion that he does not restrict to Britain.

As he told a group of Harvard students in 1981, 'America's foreign policy has been based on a fundamental misconception, the same misconception that led Carthage into misunderstanding and then succumbing to Rome. Carthage was a mercantile society which tried to interpret events in terms of trade, logic and mutual interest. Rome was an imperial power. Its purpose was to expand its empire by conquest ... Moscow is imperial. Its whole system is geared to imperial conquest. The idea that we can develop a long-term and harmonious relationship with Russia by trade and commerce has been revealed as totally naive.' It is the conclusion of a man who is used to financial conquest and who fights back as soon as he defines a threat; the attitude of someone who cannot be categorized in the traditional political pigeonholes.

He relishes the sensual pleasures. His suits are tailored in London and he consumes his food with a speed worthy of a Turk. 'He eats like a wolf and he can steal the food from your plate if he likes the look of it,' is how one of his friends puts it. He certainly likes to order his food first even if he is the host, and to eat it as soon as it is put in front of him. There are none of the nineteenth-century delicacies. He is too much of a tribal chieftain for that, which is perhaps why he is not particularly keen to be invited to anyone else's house or table. He prefers to remain the host.

There is even a strain of misogyny in him. 'Generally Jimmy considers women less intelligent, not to say more stupid than men,' Madame Beaux believes; although for his part he insists that 'if you want to understand me you should speak to the women in my life.' Certainly there is a wife and family both in Paris and in London, just as there is now a companion in New York, Laura Boulay de la Meurthe, who is thirty. He makes no secret of her existence any more than he proclaims it, which undeniably infuriates those with more conventional lives.

'He lives his life in compartments,' is how more than one of his friends explain it. 'But I could not exist in any other way,' he says openly. There are friends and family in every city he goes to regularly. Besides he believes the modern attitude to divorce is mistaken. 'The vertical polygamy practised in the West is ridiculous. The custom is that if you divorce you abandon your wife. That is pure moral turpitude. I do not agree with it and I never have.' He goes on, 'Not one iota of my relationship with Ginette has changed since our divorce. Nothing at all.' It is said with the confidence of a man who does not object to being described as larger than life, or exaggerated, and who does not object to the judgement of one friend, 'You could say he is saner than you or I, after all most people would like to have what he has, but that does not mean it's exactly normal.'

'A middle-class figure would always resent me,' he says fiercely, 'but the Governor of the Bank of England or the ordinary working man might like me.'

Jimmy Goldsmith also does not object to being called a gambler. 'A gambler knows when to play his luck and when not to, when to keep on and when to give up, and that is a good thing for a businessman!' But like many gamblers he is also both determined and secretive. 'He will do anything he needs to to win at something he decides to do,' is one judgement of him, and so little does he approve of what he once described as the 'see-through society' that he believes in keeping his intentions opaque from almost everyone. He tends to give everyone as little warning of his movements as he can, including his wife or his two principal secretaries in London and Paris.

He is also inclined to lose his temper with a Tartar's violence, although rarely over an important issue. He can throw a plate of food out of the window and he plays tennis now with sometimes extraordinary violence, but in his business affairs he shows considerable restraint, and a legendary charm. Only if he is very angry indeed do his eyes seem to turn a slightly darker blue, and his smile becomes a little more chill.

Jimmy Goldsmith seldom forgets an insult. He has a formidable memory and a massive appetite for documents.

He prepares for negotiations with such ferocious intensity, and such attention to detail, that it has led to accusations of bombast. But he knows of no other way. He does not believe, however, in keeping either grudges or documents. Once he has read or dealt with something it will be torn up and thrown on to the floor, although these days a man is detailed to collect the crumpled and torn pieces of paper once he has finished. For Jimmy Goldsmith also does not leave a great deal to chance. Some might call him impetuous, he prefers to describe himself as decisive.

If anyone asks this unquiet and restless man, who seems possessed by a demon few can understand, but who carries pictures of his children around with him in a tiny silver case, who rarely wears a watch and almost never carries money, how rich he is, he tends only to laugh.

'I have no idea,' he is fond of saying. 'If you have a few shares you can look up their value in the paper and see what you're worth. But I don't just own a few shares. I have large holdings and entire companies. So my shares are worth only what I could sell the company for, and that is a very different thing.'

Few would deny that Jimmy Goldsmith is now as rich as a mongul emperor, and he has a retinue of four personal advisers led by a former British tax inspector with a Porsche sports car to prove it. Estimates of his wealth vary from £25 million to £200 million, but none of his friends doubt that not only is he now almost unimaginably rich, but that he wishes to become even richer. 'Even if he lost it all today he would start again tomorrow,' is how one puts it.

That perhaps is the single remaining clue to his character. For although he might dream of becoming the richest man in the world, almost more important is the risk of failure. That brings him a sense of being alive. With a remark that could well have been uttered outside the tent of Tamerlane, he says firmly, 'If the next takeover comes off I could be as rich as Croesus, or I might be as poor as Job.'

Index

Robert Roberts

A RAGGED SCHOOLING

Life was harsh indeed in the tightly packed streets of industrial Salford in the years before the First World War. As he showed in his much acclaimed *The Classic Slum*, Robert Roberts knew at first hand the poverty and degradation which drove working men to seek oblivion from a pint glass, and their wives to pawn the family's Sunday best to buy bread.

But in the shadow of the factory chimneys a child could – and did – lead a life of tremendous vitality and excitement: games in the street and by the canal, daring excursions to mysterious foreign parts a mile or two down the road, flickering fantasies at the 'By Joe' cinema, the first whispered instruction in the dark pleasures of the flesh.

In this intimate and perceptive autobiography, Robert Roberts reveals the full texture and character of city life seen through the eyes of a child in the early years of the century. It is a remarkable piece of living history.

'The autobiography of an exceptional man . . . a memoir of quite extraordinary richness' – Paul Bailey, *Observer*

'A marvellous piece of work . . . this vivid portrait of a vanished community . . . bubbles with comic vitality' – Benny Green, *Spectator*

'Moving and enthralling . . . filled with humour, hope and human warmth' – Michael Kennedy, *Daily Telegraph*

'One of the best and most sensitive of English working-class autobiographies' – W. L. Webb, *Guardian*